WHAT IS THE BOOK OF ESTHER?

Kids' Guides to God's Word Series

What Is the Book of

ESTHER?

Michael Whitworth

START2FINISH

ISBN 978-1-971767-10-9

Published by Start2Finish
Bend, Oregon 97702
start2finish.org

Printed in the United States of America

30 29 28 27 26   1 2 3 4 5

For my cousin Esther—

Like your namesake, may you always be a bright light in the darkness and embody faith, courage, and wisdom.

CONTENTS

INTRODUCTION

Have you ever watched a movie where God seems completely absent? Not a movie that's against God—just one where nobody mentions him. The characters face impossible situations. They make hard choices. Things work out in ways that feel almost miraculous. But nobody prays on screen. Nobody quotes Scripture. Nobody says, "God told me to do this."

And yet, somehow, you can still sense that something bigger is going on. The timing is too perfect. The "coincidences" are too convenient. The villain's plan falls apart in ways that feel almost … orchestrated.

That's the book of Esther.

In the entire Bible, Esther is the only book that never mentions God. Not once. No one prays (at least not out loud). No one prophesies. No miracles happen—no seas part, no fire falls from heaven, no angels appear. It reads more like a political thriller than a religious text.

And yet it's one of the most important books in Scripture. Because Esther shows us something we desperately need to see: how God works when you can't see him working.

A BOOK FOR DARK TIMES

The story takes place about one hundred years after the Babylonians destroyed Jerusalem and dragged the Jewish people into exile. By now, Babylon has fallen and Persia rules the world. Some Jews have returned to rebuild Jerusalem, but most stayed behind in Persia—including a young orphan girl named Esther and her older cousin Mordecai.

These aren't the glory days of Israel. There's no temple where God's presence dwells. There's no king descended from David. There's no prophet thundering "Thus says the LORD." The Jews are scattered across a pagan empire, far from home, trying to survive under foreign rule.

It would have been easy to think God had abandoned them.

And then a crisis hits. A powerful official named Haman convinces the king to sign a decree: on a certain day, every Jew in the empire can be legally killed and their property taken. Men, women, children—everyone. It's genocide, authorized by the government, scheduled eleven months in advance.

The Jews have no army. They have no political power. They have no way to fight back.

What they do have is a queen who's been hiding her Jewish identity—and a cousin who believes she might have come to her position "for such a time as this."

WHAT YOU'RE ABOUT TO READ

The book of Esther tells the story of how the Jewish people survived. But it's not a simple rescue story. It's a tale of palace intrigue, dangerous secrets, careful strategy, and perfect timing. It's about what happens when ordinary people find themselves in extraordinary situations and have to decide who they really are.

The first chapter sets the stage in the Persian court—a world of unimaginable wealth, ridiculous excess, and fragile male egos. King Xerxes throws a six-month party to show off his empire, then demands that his queen parade her beauty before his drunk guests. When she refuses, he banishes her. The most powerful man in the world can conquer nations but can't handle his wife saying no.

Chapters 2–3 introduce our main characters. Esther, the Jewish orphan, gets swept into the king's harem and eventually becomes queen—but keeps her identity hidden. Her cousin Mordecai works at the palace gate and uncovers an assassination plot, but receives no reward. Meanwhile, a man named Haman rises to become the second most powerful person in the empire. When Mordecai refuses to bow to him, Haman decides to destroy not just Mordecai but every Jew in the world.

Chapters 4–5 bring the crisis to a head. Mordecai challenges Esther to reveal her identity and plead for her people—even though approaching the king uninvited could mean death. Esther agrees, but first asks all the Jews to fast for three days. Then she puts on her royal robes and begins a careful plan to expose Haman.

Chapters 6–7 contain the great reversal. On a night when the king can't sleep, he discovers that Mordecai was never rewarded for saving his life. Through a series of almost comically perfect coincidences, Haman ends up publicly honoring the man he planned to kill. Then, at Esther's banquet, the truth comes out. Haman is exposed and executed on the very cruci-fixion pole he built for Mordecai.

Chapters 8–10 deal with the aftermath. Haman is dead, but his decree still stands—Persian law cannot be revoked. So Mordecai writes a new decree allowing the Jews to defend themselves. When the appointed day comes, the Jews triumph over their enemies. The victory becomes an annual celebration called Purim, which Jewish communities still observe today.

WHY THIS BOOK MATTERS

You might wonder why a book that never mentions God made it into the Bible at all. Some people in ancient times wondered the same thing. But here's what they eventually understood—and what you'll see as you read:

God doesn't have to be named to be present. The book of Esther is full of "coincidences" that aren't coincidental at all. Esther happens to be beautiful. She happens to become queen. Mordecai happens to overhear an assassination plot. The king happens to have a sleepless night at exactly the right moment. Haman happens to arrive at the palace just when the king needs advice about honoring someone. None of this is luck. It's providence—God working through ordinary events to accomplish his purposes.

Faith sometimes means acting without certainty. Esther doesn't get a promise from God that everything will work out. She doesn't hear a voice from heaven telling her what to do. She has to make hard choices based on incomplete informa-tion and trust that somehow, things will work out. That's what faith looks like for most of us, most of the time.

Identity matters more than safety. For years, Esther hid who she really was. It kept her safe—but it also kept her silent when her people needed her. The turning point comes when she decides to identify with her people even though it might cost her everything. Sometimes the safest choice isn't the right choice.

Evil often destroys itself. Haman's pride leads directly to his downfall. The pole he builds for Mordecai becomes the instrument of his own execution. The day he chose for destruction becomes a day of deliverance. Throughout Scripture, we see this pattern: evil overreaches and collapses under its own weight.

God's purposes will not fail. Mordecai tells Esther that if she stays silent, "relief and deliverance for the Jews will arise from another place." He's confident—not in Esther, but in God. He knows that God has made promises to his people that he will keep, no matter what. That confidence enables him to act with courage instead of despair.

BEFORE YOU READ

A few things to keep in mind:

The Persian court was extravagant beyond anything you've experienced. When the book describes gold and silver couches, marble floors, and six-month parties, it's not exaggerating. Archaeological discoveries have confirmed that Persian kings really did live like this. The excess is intentional—it shows us the kind of world Esther had to navigate.

The morality is complicated. Esther hides her identity. Mordecai seems proud. The violence at the end is troubling. The book doesn't present its characters as perfect role models. It presents them as real people making difficult choices in impossible circumstances—and it shows how God worked through them anyway.

The book is surprisingly funny. There's dark humor throughout—the pompous king, the oblivious officials, Haman's spectacular humiliation. The author wants you to laugh at the absurdity of human pride and the ways God turns human schemes upside down.

This points to something bigger. The deliverance in Esther was real, but it was also temporary. The Jews still lived in a pagan empire. They still faced future threats. The book points forward to a greater deliverance—one that would come through another descendant of Abraham who would save his people not from a Persian decree but from sin and death itself.

THE STORY BEGINS

So here we are, about to enter the palace of the most powerful king on earth. We'll meet a queen who loses everything because she says no and an orphan who gains everything because she says yes. We'll watch a villain rise and fall. We'll see what happens when ordinary people trust an invisible God.

The name of God never appears in this book.

But by the end, you won't be able to miss him.

Turn the page.

1

THE PARTY THAT CHANGED EVERYTHING

In the movie *Aladdin*, there's a moment when the villain Jafar finally gets what he's always wanted: ultimate power. He uses the genie's magic to become the most powerful sorcerer in the world. Then he becomes sultan. And then—because it's still not enough—he wishes to become an all-powerful genie himself. "The universe is mine to command!" he shouts, as cosmic power flows through him.

But here's the thing Jafar didn't think through: genies have to live in lamps. The very power he craved becomes his prison. He gets sucked into a tiny bronze lamp, trapped forever. The guy who wanted to control everything ends up controlling nothing.

That's basically the book of Esther in miniature.

It's a story about powerful people who think they're in charge—kings and queens, nobles and advisors, people who can command armies and change laws with a word. But throughout the whole book, you'll watch their carefully laid plans backfire, their schemes collapse, their power turn into weakness. And quietly, behind all of it, someone else is actually in control.

That someone is never named. In fact, here's the strangest thing about the book of Esther: God is never mentioned. Not once. No prayers are recorded. No prophets speak. No miracles flash across the sky. If you're reading quickly, you might think God has nothing to do with this story at all.

But that's exactly the point.

The book of Esther is about how God works when you can't see him working. It's about providence—that behind-the-scenes activity of God where he guides events toward his purposes without announcing what he's doing. It's about learning to trust that God is present even when he seems absent.

And it all begins with a party.

WHERE ARE WE?

Before we dive into the story, we need to understand where we are in history. Remember the story of Israel? After centuries of kings—some good, most bad—God's people were conquered. Babylon destroyed Jerusalem in 586 BC. The temple was demolished. The people were carried off into exile.

But then Babylon fell to Persia in 539 BC. The new Persian king, Cyrus, let the Jews go home and even helped them rebuild their temple.

Some Jews returned to Jerusalem. That's the story told in Ezra and Nehemiah. But here's what's easy to miss: most Jews didn't go back. The exile had lasted seventy years. By the time Cyrus issued his decree, generations had grown up in Babylon and Persia. They had jobs, homes, families, and lives.

So while some Jews returned to rebuild Jerusalem, huge numbers stayed scattered throughout the Persian Empire, trying to stay faithful to God while living as a tiny minority in a pagan world.

That's the world of Esther. The story takes place in Susa, one of the capital cities of the Persian Empire, during the reign of a king named Xerxes (the Hebrew form of his name is Ahasuerus). It's about fifty years after Cyrus first let the Jews go home. The temple in Jerusalem has been rebuilt, but most Jews are still living far from the promised land. And one of those Jews is a young woman named Esther.

But she doesn't appear yet. First, we have to meet the king.

THE KING'S PARTY

The book opens with a display of power so over-the-top it's almost comical: "In the days of Ahasuerus, the Ahasuerus who reigned from India to Ethiopia over 127 provinces, in those days when King Ahasuerus sat on his royal throne in Susa the citadel, in the third year of his reign he gave a feast for all his officials and servants. The army of Persia and Media and the nobles and governors of the provinces were before him, while he showed the riches of his royal glory and the splendor and pomp of his greatness for many days, 180 days."

Read that last part again. He showed off his wealth and glory for 180 days. That's six months. Half a year of "look how amazing I am." The author wants you to feel the weight of this empire. From India to Ethiopia. 127 provinces. The army chiefs of Persia and Media. Nobles and governors from across the known world gathered to gaze upon the king's magnificence.

Why such an elaborate display? History tells us this banquet probably coincided with Xerxes' planning for his invasion of Greece. He needed to rally support from leaders across his empire, convince them to send troops and treasure for his military campaign. What better way to inspire confidence than to show off just how wealthy and powerful he already was?

But there's something else going on here. The author isn't just describing Persian power—he's subtly mocking it. The repetition of "king" and "royal" in almost every sentence, the absurd length of the party, the exhausting list of titles and territories—it's all a bit much. Like someone who brags so loudly that you start to wonder what they're compensating for.

After the six-month showcase for the VIPs, the king threw another party: "And when these days were completed, the king gave for all the people present in Susa the citadel, both great and small, a feast lasting for seven days in the court of the garden of the king's palace."

Try to picture this scene. White and blue fabric draped everywhere, caught up with purple cords on silver rings attached to marble columns. Gold and silver couches arranged on a floor made of precious stones. Wine flowing freely in golden cups, each one unique, because apparently even the drinking vessels needed to show off the king's wealth.

This wasn't just a party. It was a statement. It said, "I am so rich, so powerful, so magnificent that I can afford all of this without even noticing the expense. Everything in Persia belongs to me, and I can do whatever I want with it."

The text adds one more detail about the drinking: "Drinking was according to this edict: 'No one is compelled.' For the king had given orders to all the staff of his palace to do as each man desired." That sounds generous, doesn't it? Normally at

Persian royal banquets, when the king drank, everyone had to drink. It was protocol. But Xerxes was being magnanimous— drink if you want, don't drink if you don't want. No pressure!

Except here's the irony: in a few verses, the king will be absolutely enraged when someone exercises the same kind of choice about something far more important than wine. "Do as you desire" only works when people desire what the king wants them to desire.

THE QUEEN'S REFUSAL

While all this was happening, Queen Vashti was hosting her own banquet for the women in another part of the palace. The text doesn't tell us much about her party—it wasn't about her anyway. Everything in Persia was about the king.

And on the seventh day of the feast, when the king was feeling very good from all that royal wine, he got an idea: "On the seventh day, when the heart of the king was merry with wine, he commanded the seven eunuchs who served in the presence of King Ahasuerus to bring Queen Vashti before the king with her royal crown, in order to show the peoples and the princes her beauty, for she was lovely to look at."

Seven servants—even his errand-runners came in impressive numbers—were sent to fetch the queen. The king wanted to display her to his guests, just like he'd displayed his golden cups and marble pillars and violet hangings. She was beautiful, after all. Why not add her to the exhibition?

Stop and feel how degrading this was. Vashti wasn't being invited to the party as a guest. She was being summoned as an object—another piece of royal property to show off to a bunch of drunk men. "Look at my wealth. Look at my palace. Look at my wife. Isn't she pretty?"

Some ancient interpreters thought the command was even worse than it sounds—that "with her royal crown" meant she was supposed to appear wearing *only* the crown. We can't know for sure if that's what was intended, but even the most generous reading of the command has the king treating his queen like a trophy.

Vashti said no. That's it. No speech, no explanation, no dramatic confrontation. Just a simple refusal. The queen would not be paraded before drunken party guests for their entertainment. It's one of the boldest acts of defiance in the entire Bible. Vashti had to know the risk. You didn't refuse the king of Persia. His word was law—literally. The same man who could throw a six-month party could have someone executed with a snap of his fingers. But she refused anyway. She chose her dignity over her safety.

The king's reaction tells us everything we need to know about his character: "At this the king became enraged, and his anger burned within him."

Remember, this is the most powerful man in the known world. He rules from India to Ethiopia. Armies march at his command. Nations tremble at his frown. And he has just been publicly humiliated by his own wife at his own party in front of all his important guests. His heart may have been "merry with wine" a moment ago, but now it's burning with rage.

A LAW FOR ALL THE LAND

What happens next would be funny if it weren't so revealing.

The king calls a meeting. Not just any meeting—he consults his top advisors, "wise men who knew the times," the seven nobles who had direct access to the king. These were the most powerful men in the empire after Xerxes himself.

And here's the question the king of Persia brings before this august assembly: "According to the law, what is to be done to Queen Vashti, because she has not performed the command of King Ahasuerus delivered by the eunuchs?"

Think about this. The ruler of 127 provinces, commander of the mightiest army on earth, needs to ask his advisors what to do because his wife embarrassed him at a party. The man who wanted everyone to see how great he was just revealed how small he really is.

One of the advisors, Memucan, steps forward with his analysis of the situation. And his response is absolutely absurd: "Not only against the king has Queen Vashti done wrong, but also against all the officials and all the peoples who are in all the provinces of King Ahasuerus. For the queen's behavior will be made known to all women, causing them to look at their husbands with contempt, since they will say, 'King Ahasuerus commanded Queen Vashti to be brought before him, and she did not come.' This very day the noble women of Persia and Media who have heard of the queen's behavior will say the same to all the king's officials, and there will be contempt and wrath in plenty."

Do you see what's happening? A domestic dispute between a husband and wife has been inflated into a national crisis. Memucan is essentially arguing, "If we let this stand, wives everywhere will start disobeying their husbands! We'll have contempt and wrath in every household from India to Ethiopia! The very fabric of society will unravel!"

It's ridiculous. And the proposed solution is even more ridiculous: "If it please the king, let a royal order go out from him, and let it be written among the laws of the Persians and the Medes so that it may not be repealed, that Vashti is never again to come before King Ahasuerus. And let the king give her royal position to another who is better than she. So when the decree made by the king is proclaimed throughout all his kingdom, for it is vast, all women will give honor to their husbands, high and low alike."

The king and his nobles love this idea. It's a face-saving measure dressed up as public policy. So letters go out to every province, in every language, proclaiming that "every man be master in his own household."

Here's the thing: that decree accomplished nothing. You can't legislate respect. If a husband needs a royal decree to get his wife to listen to him, he's already lost. The law just made the king look foolish—and made sure everyone in the empire heard about Vashti's defiance.

The author of Esther wants us to notice how ridiculous all of this is. The great king of Persia, with all his wealth and power, can't handle a disagreement with his wife without mobilizing the entire apparatus of state. His "wise men" give him terrible advice. His unchangeable law is laughably petty. The more he tries to assert his authority, the more obvious it becomes that his authority is fragile.

And here's what's really ironic: by banishing Vashti and declaring that her position will go to "another who is better,"

Memucan has just set the stage for everything that follows. He thinks he's solving a problem. Actually, he's creating an opening for a Jewish orphan girl to become queen of Persia.

The powerful men in the room have no idea what they've just set in motion. But someone else does.

WHAT THIS MEANS FOR US

First, true power isn't what it looks like. Xerxes had everything—wealth, armies, an empire spanning continents. But when his wife refused a demeaning request, he fell apart. He needed advisors to tell him what to do. He needed laws to prop up his authority. All that outward power masked an inner weakness.

We live in a world that's impressed by the same things that impressed the ancient Persians: money, status, influence, and control. But the book of Esther is going to show us that real power works differently. The people who seem to be in charge often aren't. The people who seem powerless often have more influence than anyone realizes. And behind it all, there's a God who doesn't need to show off because his authority doesn't depend on anyone else's recognition.

Second, doing the right thing can be costly—and still be right. Vashti refused to be degraded, and it cost her everything. She lost her position, her access to the king, and probably her lifestyle. The text doesn't tell us she was vindicated or that things worked out for her. Sometimes doing the right thing doesn't come with a happy ending, at least not one we get to see.

But her refusal mattered. It was an act of dignity in a world that wanted to treat her as an object. And it created the opening through which God would work his plan. Vashti probably never knew the role her courage played in saving the Jewish people. Sometimes our faithfulness plants seeds we'll never see grow.

Third, God is working even when he's silent. This is the biggest theme in Esther, and we see hints of it already. God isn't mentioned in this chapter. There are no miracles, no prophets, and no divine announcements. Just palace politics and petty human drama.

But look at what happened: through a king's vanity, a queen's courage, and an advisor's foolish counsel, a position opened up that would eventually be filled by a Jewish woman. When the crisis comes—and it's coming—God will have his person in exactly the right place.

That's how providence works. It's rarely dramatic. It usually looks like ordinary events unfolding in ordinary ways. But when you step back and see the whole picture, you realize that nothing was random. The God who seems absent is actually working through every detail.

Fourth, human plans often backfire. Xerxes threw a party to show how powerful he was—and ended up looking weak. He issued a decree to establish his authority—and made himself a laughingstock. Memucan tried to solve one problem— and created the conditions for something far bigger than he could imagine.

This pattern will repeat throughout Esther. Characters will scheme and plot and think they're in control, and their schemes will collapse or produce results they never intended. It's one of the ways the book reminds us that there's a higher script being written than the one humans think they're writing.

TALKING POINTS

Here are some points for you to think about and discuss:

1. **Xerxes displayed his wealth and power for six months to impress his guests.** What are some ways people today try to impress others with what they have or who they are? Why do you think we're tempted to do this?

2. **Vashti refused to be treated as an object, even though it cost her everything.** Can you think of a time when doing the right thing might cost you something significant? What makes it hard to choose dignity over safety?

3. **The book of Esther never mentions God by name.** Why do you think the author chose to tell the story this way? What might it teach us about how God works in our own lives?

4. **Memucan's advice seemed to solve the king's problem but actually set up everything that would happen next.** How have you seen situations where human plans ended up leading somewhere completely unexpected?

5. **The king and his advisors thought they were the ones in control of this story.** Who do you think is really in control? What evidence would you point to?

The party is over. The decree has been sent. Vashti is gone. Somewhere in Susa, a young Jewish woman named Hadassah has no idea that her life is about to change forever.

Turn the page.

2

AN ORPHAN IN THE PALACE

In the movie *Cinderella*, there's a moment when everything changes for a girl nobody noticed. She's been living in the shadows, doing what she's told, invisible to everyone who matters. She has no parents to advocate for her, no money to buy her way into high society, no connections to open doors. She's just a servant girl scrubbing floors while her stepsisters prepare for the royal ball.

Then comes the invitation. Every eligible young woman in the kingdom is summoned to the palace. The prince is looking for a bride. And somehow—through a series of events that seem like pure luck but feel like something more—this invisible girl ends up dancing with the most powerful person in the land. By the end of the night, everything has changed.

It's a fairy tale, of course. But fairy tales often echo deeper truths. And in the book of Esther, we find a story that mirrors Cinderella in surprising ways—except this one actually happened. And instead of a fairy godmother working behind the scenes, there's someone far more powerful.

THE KING'S REGRET

Some time after Vashti's banishment, the king started having second thoughts. "After these things, when the anger of King Xerxes had abated, he remembered Vashti and what she had done and what had been decreed against her."

Notice what's happening here. The anger has cooled. The wine has worn off. And now Xerxes is thinking clearly—maybe for the first time since that disastrous party. He remembers Vashti. He remembers what she did. And he remembers what he did in response.

The text doesn't say he missed her, but it's hard to read this any other way. He's trapped by his own decision. Remember those unchangeable laws of the Medes and Persians? The very decree that was supposed to show how powerful the king was has now become his prison. He can't bring Vashti back even if he wants to.

How much time passed between chapter 1 and chapter 2? More than you might think. History tells us that during these years, Xerxes was away from Susa, fighting a disastrous war against Greece. He invaded with one of the largest armies ever assembled—and got crushed. The famous battles of Thermopylae (where three hundred Spartans held off the Persian army) and Salamis (where the Greek navy destroyed the Persian fleet) happened during this period.

So when we read that the king "remembered Vashti," we're seeing a defeated man returning home. His military ambitions have been humiliated. His treasury is depleted. His reputation is damaged. And now he's lonely.

The servants noticed. And they had an idea.

THE SEARCH FOR A NEW QUEEN

"Then the king's personal attendants proposed, 'Let a search be made for beautiful young virgins for the king. Let the king appoint commissioners in every province of his realm to bring all these beautiful young women into the harem at the citadel of Susa. Let them be placed under the care of Hegai, the king's eunuch, who is in charge of the women; and let beauty treatments be given to them. Then let the young woman who pleases the king be queen instead of Vashti.' This advice appealed to the king, and he followed it."

Read that carefully. The servants are proposing to search all 127 provinces of the empire to find every beautiful young woman and bring them to Susa. This isn't a beauty contest where girls sign up hoping to win a crown. This is a draft.

We need to be honest about what's happening here, because the Bible doesn't pretend it was romantic. Young women from across the empire were taken from their homes and families, brought to the capital, and placed in the king's harem. Most of them would spend the rest of their lives there, rarely if ever seeing the king again after their one night with him. They couldn't go home. They couldn't marry anyone else. They were, in effect, prisoners in a gilded cage.

This is the world Esther lived in. It wasn't fair. It wasn't kind. It was the brutal reality of life under an absolute monarch who believed everything and everyone in his empire existed for his pleasure.

And somewhere in Susa, a Jewish orphan girl was about to get swept up in it.

MEET THE FAMILY

Before Esther appears, the author introduces us to her cousin: "Now there was in the citadel of Susa a Jew of the tribe of Benjamin, named Mordecai son of Jair, the son of Shimei, the son of Kish, who had been carried into exile from Jerusalem by Nebuchadnezzar king of Babylon, among those taken captive with Jehoiachin king of Judah."

Why does this genealogy matter? Because the author wants us to know exactly who Mordecai is and where he comes from. He's a Jew—one of God's chosen people living far from the promised land. He's from the tribe of Benjamin—the same tribe as Israel's first king, Saul. And his ancestor Kish shares a name with Saul's father. The author is connecting Mordecai to royal bloodlines, hinting that this seemingly ordinary man has a heritage more significant than his current circumstances suggest.

The mention of the exile is important too. Mordecai's family had been carried away from Jerusalem when Babylon conquered Judah. Now, generations later, they're still living in foreign territory—no longer in Babylon, but in Persia, which had conquered Babylon. They're exiles within an exile, strangers in a strange land.

And Mordecai had a cousin: "Mordecai had a cousin named Hadassah, whom he had brought up because she had neither father nor mother. This young woman, who was also known as Esther, was lovely in form and features, and Mordecai had taken her as his own daughter when her father and mother died."

Esther was an orphan. We don't know how her parents died or how old she was when it happened. What we know is that Mordecai stepped in. He didn't just help out or keep an eye on her—he "took her as his own daughter." He adopted her. He raised her. He gave her a family when she had lost hers.

She had two names. Her Hebrew name was Hadassah, which means "myrtle"—a flowering shrub that symbolized peace and God's blessing in Jewish tradition. Her Persian name was Esther, which sounds like the word for "star" and is related to the name of the Babylonian goddess Ishtar. The double name suggests someone living between two worlds, navigating both Jewish identity and Persian culture.

And she was beautiful. The text emphasizes this twice: "lovely in form and features." In a story where the king is searching for beautiful young women, this detail matters. Esther's beauty will catch the attention of powerful people—for better or worse.

TAKEN TO THE PALACE

"When the king's order and edict had been proclaimed, many young women were brought to the citadel of Susa and put under the care of Hegai. Esther also was taken to the king's palace and entrusted to Hegai, who had charge of the harem." Notice the passive language: Esther "was taken." She didn't volunteer. She didn't apply. She was collected like the others—swept up in the empire's machinery.

Try to imagine this from her perspective. One day you're living with your cousin, the only family you have left. The next day, soldiers or officials come to your door. They're gathering beautiful young women for the king. You fit the description. You have no choice.

Suddenly you're in the palace, surrounded by strangers, cut off from everyone you know. You're being prepared for a night with a man you've never met—a pagan king who just divorced his wife for refusing to be put on display. Your entire future depends on whether you can please him.

This wasn't a fairy tale. It was terrifying.

But something strange happened: "The young woman pleased [Hegai] and won his favor. Immediately he provided her with her beauty treatments and special food. He assigned to her seven female attendants selected from the king's palace and moved her and her attendants into the best place in the harem."

Hegai was the official in charge of the harem—a powerful position in the Persian court. And for some reason, he immediately favored Esther. He gave her special treatment: the best beauty preparations, the best food, seven personal attendants, the best rooms in the harem.

Why? The text doesn't say Esther did anything to earn this. She just "won his favor." It happened to her.

This is one of the most important patterns in the book of Esther. Things keep happening *to* Esther that position her for what's coming. She doesn't scheme or manipulate her way to the top. Favor just seems to find her.

In a book that never mentions God by name, this is one of the ways the author hints at providence. Someone is working behind the scenes, arranging circumstances, and opening doors. Esther finds favor not because she's trying to—but because God is positioning his person for his purposes.

A HIDDEN IDENTITY

There's one more detail in this section that will become crucial later: "Esther had not revealed her nationality and family background, because Mordecai had forbidden her to do so. Every day he walked back and forth near the courtyard of the harem to find out how Esther was and what was happening to her." Mordecai told Esther to hide the fact that she was Jewish. And she obeyed.

Why the secrecy? The text doesn't explain, but we can guess. Jews were a minority in the Persian Empire—outsiders, foreigners, people with different customs and different loyalties. Revealing her identity might have disqualified her or made her a target. Keeping quiet was a survival strategy.

But it also created a tension. Esther was living as if she were Persian while actually being Jewish. She was hiding the most important thing about herself—her identity as one of God's people.

Was this right? Was it wrong? The author doesn't tell us. He simply reports it and lets the story unfold. What we can see is that Esther's hidden identity will matter enormously later. The very thing she's concealing will become the thing that positions her to save her people.

Meanwhile, Mordecai kept watch. Every day he walked near the harem courtyard, trying to learn how his adopted daughter was doing. He couldn't speak to her directly, but he refused to forget her. Even though she'd been taken into a world he couldn't enter, he stayed as close as he could.

TWELVE MONTHS OF PREPARATION

The author now explains what happened to the young women

in the harem: "Before a young woman's turn came to go in to King Xerxes, she had to complete twelve months of beauty treatments prescribed for the women, six months with oil of myrrh and six months with perfumes and cosmetics."

A full year of preparation before meeting the king. Six months of treatment with myrrh oil. Six months with other perfumes and cosmetics. It's almost absurd—the amount of time and resources devoted to making these women physically appealing to one man.

But it also reveals something about Persian values. Appearance mattered more than character. External beauty received a year of investment; no one asked about wisdom, kindness, or integrity.

After the twelve months: "When she went to the king, she was given whatever she wanted to take with her from the harem to the king's palace. In the evening she would go there and in the morning return to another part of the harem to the care of Shaashgaz, the king's eunuch who was in charge of the concubines. She would not return to the king unless he was pleased with her and summoned her by name."

Each woman got one night. She could take whatever she wanted—jewelry, clothes, anything she thought might help her succeed. Then she went to the king. In the morning, she was moved to a different part of the harem, the section for concubines. Unless the king specifically called for her again, she would live out her days there—technically married to the king but essentially abandoned.

It's a grim picture. Hundreds of young women, each given one chance, then set aside and forgotten. The vast majority would never see the king again. They'd given up their freedom, their futures, their chance at a normal life—and received almost nothing in return.

ESTHER'S TURN

Finally, after years in the harem, Esther's turn came: "When the turn came for Esther (the young woman Mordecai had adopted, the daughter of his uncle Abihail) to go to the king, she asked for nothing other than what Hegai, the king's eunuch who was in charge of the harem, suggested."

This detail is significant. The other women loaded themselves down with whatever they thought might impress the king. Esther took only what Hegai recommended. She trusted his judgment rather than her own desires.

It's a small thing, but it reveals character. Esther wasn't grasping or greedy. She wasn't trying to manipulate the situation. She simply listened to wise counsel and followed it.

And then, that familiar pattern again: "Esther won the favor of everyone who saw her." Not just Hegai. Not just the king. *Everyone.* Wherever Esther went, favor followed.

The date is given precisely: "the tenth month, which is the month of Tebeth, in the seventh year of his reign." That's the winter of 479 BC—four years after Vashti was deposed. The search had taken that long.

And then: "Now the king was attracted to Esther more than to any of the other women, and she won his favor and approval more than any of the other virgins. So he set a royal crown on her head and made her queen instead of Vashti."

After years of searching, after hundreds of young women

had passed through, the king chose Esther. The orphan girl from a Jewish family became queen of the Persian Empire.

The king threw another party—"Esther's banquet"—and declared a holiday throughout the provinces. He gave gifts with royal generosity. The empire celebrated its new queen.

And almost nobody knew who she really was.

WHAT THIS MEANS FOR US

First, God positions his people for his purposes. Esther didn't choose to be beautiful. She didn't choose to be taken to the palace. She didn't scheme her way to the throne. Step by step, circumstances moved her toward a position she never sought—and that position would later become the means of saving her people.

Sometimes we find ourselves in situations we didn't choose and don't understand. A job we didn't expect. A school we didn't plan on. A neighborhood, a relationship, a circumstance that just happened to us. It's worth asking: what if God has placed me here for a reason I can't see yet?

Second, favor is often God's fingerprint on our lives. The repeated emphasis on Esther finding favor points to something beyond luck or charm. When doors open that we didn't push on, when people help us for reasons we can't explain, when circumstances align in ways we couldn't have arranged—that's often providence at work.

This doesn't mean everything good that happens is from God or that we should expect constant favor. But it does mean we should pay attention when it happens and hold it loosely, asking: what might God be doing through this?

Third, difficult circumstances don't disqualify us from God's plans. Esther was an orphan, an exile, a young woman with no power in a world ruled by powerful men. She was taken into a morally compromising situation she didn't choose. None of that disqualified her from being used by God.

If you feel stuck in circumstances that seem wrong or unfair, if you're dealing with the consequences of others' choices or your own past mistakes, know this: God is not limited by your situation. He specializes in working through people who seem to have everything against them.

Fourth, obedience in small things prepares us for bigger moments. Esther obeyed Mordecai by hiding her identity. She took Hegai's advice about what to bring to the king. These seem like minor details, but they reveal a pattern of trusting wise counsel and following through. That pattern would matter enormously when the stakes got higher.

The habits you build now—listening to wisdom, doing the right thing even when no one's watching, trusting God in small decisions—those habits will shape who you are when the big moments come.

TALKING POINTS

Here are a few things to consider and talk over:

1. **Esther didn't choose her circumstances—she was taken to the palace against her will.** How do you respond when life takes you somewhere you didn't plan to go? How might God use unchosen circumstances?

2. **Mordecai told Esther to hide her Jewish identity.** Do you think this was the right decision? What might have

happened if she had been open about who she was from the very beginning??

3. **Esther kept finding "favor" with everyone she met.** What do you think this means? Can you think of times in your own life when things worked out in ways you couldn't explain?

4. **The beauty treatments lasted twelve months—a huge investment in external appearance.** What do our culture's "beauty treatments" look like today? What gets neglected when we focus too much on the outside?

5. **Esther took only what Hegai suggested rather than loading up on jewelry and accessories.** What does this reveal about her character? How does humility help us in life?

An orphan girl now wears the crown. A Jew sits on Persia's throne, though no one knows it yet. But the story is just getting started. Because somewhere in the palace, a man named Haman is about to rise to power. And he has plans that will put everything—Esther's secret, her people, and her very life—on the line.

Turn the page.

3

THE ENEMY RISES

In *Harry Potter and the Prisoner of Azkaban*, there's a scene where Harry saves his godfather Sirius Black from the Dementors by casting a powerful Patronus spell. But here's what makes the scene complicated: Harry only knows he can cast that spell because he's already seen himself do it—thanks to time travel. When Hermione asks how he knew he could do it, Harry says, "I just knew."

But actually, something else was happening in the background. Earlier in the story, Peter Pettigrew—a man everyone thought was dead—had been exposed as alive and guilty of betraying Harry's parents to Voldemort. The evidence was right there. Justice should have been served. But then everything went wrong. Pettigrew escaped. Sirius remained a fugitive. And the villain who would later help Voldemort return to power slipped away into the night.

Sometimes stories work like that. A hero does something good—and gets nothing for it. A villain escapes justice—and rises to power. The good deed gets forgotten while the bad guy climbs higher.

That's exactly what happens in Esther 3.

A GOOD DEED FORGOTTEN

At the end of chapter 2, something important happened that's easy to overlook: "During the time Mordecai was sitting at the king's gate, Bigthana and Teresh, two of the king's officers who guarded the doorway, became angry and conspired to assassinate King Xerxes. But Mordecai found out about the plot and told Queen Esther, who in turn reported it to the king, giving credit to Mordecai. And when the report was investigated and found to be true, the two officials were impaled on poles. All this was recorded in the book of the annals in the presence of the king."

Mordecai uncovered an assassination plot. Two of the king's own guards—men trusted to protect him—were planning to kill him. Mordecai discovered their conspiracy, reported it through Esther, and saved the king's life.

This was a big deal. Persian kings were famous for rewarding people who helped them. They kept official lists of "benefactors"—people who had done favors for the king—and those people received generous rewards. Wealth, land, positions of honor—the king took care of those who took care of him.

So what did Mordecai get for saving the king's life?

Nothing.

The event was recorded in the royal chronicles—we'll come back to that later—but Mordecai received no reward, no recognition, no promotion. The man who saved the king was apparently forgotten the moment the conspirators were executed.

This seems deeply unfair. And if you're paying attention to how stories work, you might expect the next paragraph to describe Mordecai finally getting what he deserved.

Instead, we get this: "After these events, King Xerxes honored Haman son of Hammedatha, the Agagite, elevating him and giving him a seat of honor higher than that of all the other nobles."

Wait—what? Mordecai saves the king's life and gets nothing. Then some guy named Haman shows up out of nowhere and gets promoted to the highest position in the kingdom?

The author wants us to feel this injustice. He puts these two events back-to-back precisely so we'll notice how wrong it is. The man who deserved honor was overlooked. The man who would become the villain received everything.

This is one of the hardest things about life in a fallen world: sometimes evil people prosper while good people are ignored. The wicked get promoted while the faithful get passed over. It doesn't seem fair because it isn't fair.

But the story isn't over. And God has a way of using even injustice to accomplish his purposes.

MEET THE VILLAIN

So who is this Haman? The text identifies him carefully: "Haman son of Hammedatha, the Agagite." That last word—Agagite—is the key.

Remember back in 1 Samuel, when Israel had its first king? Saul was commanded by God to completely destroy the Amalekites, an enemy nation that had attacked Israel centuries earlier when they were vulnerable refugees fleeing Egypt. God said to wipe them out entirely. But Saul didn't obey. He spared Agag, the Amalekite king, along with the best of the livestock. That disobedience cost Saul his kingdom. Samuel the prophet executed Agag himself. But apparently Agag had descendants who survived.

Haman was one of them.

Now here's where it gets interesting. Remember Mordecai's genealogy from chapter 2? He was "the son of Jair, the son of Shimei, the son of Kish, a Benjaminite." Kish was the name of King Saul's father. Mordecai came from the same family line as the king who failed to destroy Agag.

So we have a descendant of Saul and a descendant of Agag, both serving in the Persian court, centuries after their ancestors' conflict. The ancient grudge between Israel and Amalek is about to explode again—this time with the survival of an entire people at stake.

Haman has been elevated above every other official in the empire. He's essentially the prime minister, second only to the king himself. And with that promotion came a command: "All the royal officials at the king's gate knelt down and paid honor to Haman, for the king had commanded this concerning him."

Everyone was required to bow when Haman passed by. It was a display of his new authority, a daily reminder that this man now held more power than anyone except the king.

Everyone bowed. Almost everyone. "But Mordecai would not kneel down or pay him honor."

THE MAN WHO WOULDN'T BOW

Why wouldn't Mordecai bow? The text doesn't explain his

reasoning directly, but it gives us a crucial detail. When the other officials asked Mordecai why he was disobeying the king's command, he told them "he was a Jew."

His Jewish identity was the reason. This might seem strange. Jews did bow to human authorities on other occasions in the Bible. There was nothing inherently wrong with showing respect to someone in power. So why couldn't Mordecai bow to Haman?

The answer probably lies in who Haman was. As an Agagite—a descendant of Israel's ancient enemy—Haman represented everything that had opposed God's people for generations. The Amalekites had attacked Israel when they were weak. They had shown no fear of God. For a Jew to bow before an Agagite would feel like a betrayal of his people and his God.

Or maybe it was something about how Haman demanded worship. The kind of honor he expected—everyone dropping to their knees as he walked by—may have crossed a line from respect into something that belonged only to God.

Whatever the exact reason, Mordecai drew a line. He would not bow. "Day after day they spoke to him but he refused to comply. Therefore they told Haman about it to see whether Mordecai's behavior would be tolerated, for he had told them he was a Jew."

The other officials were curious. They kept pressuring Mordecai, but he wouldn't budge. So they reported him to Haman, wanting to see what would happen. Would this Jew get away with his defiance?

Haman's reaction revealed his true character: "When Haman saw that Mordecai would not kneel down or pay him honor, he was enraged. Yet having learned who Mordecai's people were, he scorned the idea of killing only Mordecai. Instead Haman looked for a way to destroy all Mordecai's people, the Jews, throughout the whole kingdom of Xerxes."

Read that again. One man refused to bow—so Haman decided to kill an entire race.

This is the logic of evil. Haman's pride was wounded by one person's defiance, so he would make everyone who shared that person's identity pay. It didn't matter that most Jews had never even met Mordecai. It didn't matter that they posed no threat to Haman or the empire. One Jew had disrespected him, so all Jews must die.

This is the same twisted logic behind every genocide in history. One group decides another group must be eliminated—not because of anything individuals have done, but simply because of who they are. It happened to Jews in Persia. It happened to Jews in Nazi Germany. It has happened to countless peoples throughout history when hatred combines with power.

Haman had the hatred. Now he needed a plan.

ROLLING THE DICE

"In the twelfth year of King Xerxes, in the first month, the month of Nisan, the pur (that is, the lot) was cast in the presence of Haman to select a day and month. And the lot fell on the twelfth month, the month of Adar."

Before making his move, Haman consulted the ancient equivalent of a horoscope. He cast lots—something like rolling dice—to determine the best day for his plan. In the ancient world, people believed the gods communicated through random events like the fall of lots. By casting them, Haman was trying to find the "lucky" day for destroying the Jews.

The lot fell on the twelfth month, Adar. That was almost a year away. Haman would have to wait eleven months before his massacre could take place.

Here's what Haman didn't know: the lot may have seemed random, but it wasn't. The book of Proverbs says, "The lot is cast into the lap, but its every decision is from the LORD" (16:33). God was already at work in what looked like chance. By pushing the date so far into the future, God was giving his people time—time for the rescue plan to unfold.

This is one of the ways the book of Esther shows God's hidden hand. The villain thinks he's in control. He thinks the stars have aligned in his favor. But behind what looks like luck, God is quietly arranging circumstances for his own purposes.

THE LIE THAT KILLS

With his lucky day selected, Haman went to the king: "There is a certain people dispersed among the peoples in all the provinces of your kingdom who keep themselves separate. Their customs are different from those of all other people, and they do not obey the king's laws; it is not in the king's best interest to tolerate them. If it pleases the king, let a decree be issued to destroy them, and I will give ten thousand talents of silver to the king's treasury for the men who carry out this work."

Notice how Haman presents his case. He doesn't mention the Jews by name. He doesn't explain that this is really about one man who wounded his pride. Instead, he makes it sound like a matter of state security.

"There's this group scattered throughout your kingdom. They're different from everyone else. They have their own customs. They don't follow your laws. They're a threat to the empire. You'd be better off without them."

It was a brilliant and terrible combination of truth, half-truth, and outright lies. Yes, the Jews were scattered throughout the empire. Yes, they had their own customs. But the claim that they didn't obey the king's laws? That was false. Mordecai himself had just saved the king's life. The Jews weren't rebels or troublemakers.

But Haman knew his audience. He knew Xerxes wouldn't investigate. He knew the king would be swayed by the promise of money—ten thousand talents of silver was an astronomical sum, perhaps equivalent to billions of dollars today. And he knew the king was lazy enough to hand over authority without asking hard questions.

"So the king took his signet ring from his finger and gave it to Haman son of Hammedatha, the Agagite, the enemy of the Jews. 'Keep the money' the king said to Haman, 'and do with the people as you please.'"

The king didn't ask which people. He didn't verify Haman's claims. He just handed over his signet ring—the equivalent of giving someone your signature on a blank check—and told Haman to do whatever he wanted.

This is what happens when leaders stop leading. When those in power care more about their own comfort than about justice, evil men can manipulate them into approving monstrous things. Xerxes wasn't directly evil. He was just indifferent. And his indifference made him complicit in genocide.

THE DEATH SENTENCE

The machinery of empire swung into action: "Then on the thirteenth day of the first month the royal secretaries were summoned. They wrote out in the script of each province and in the language of each people all Haman's orders to the king's satraps, the governors of the various provinces and the nobles of the various peoples. These were written in the name of King Xerxes himself and sealed with his own ring. Dispatches were sent by couriers to all the king's provinces with the order to destroy, kill and annihilate all the Jews—young and old, women and children—on a single day, the thirteenth day of the twelfth month, the month of Adar, and to plunder their goods."

Every province received the decree. Every language carried the message. On a single day, eleven months from now, every Jew in the Persian Empire—from India to Ethiopia—was to be killed. Men, women, children. The elderly. Infants. No exceptions.

The date chosen was the thirteenth of Adar. Notice something the original readers would have caught immediately: the decree was issued on the thirteenth of Nisan. The very next day, the fourteenth of Nisan, was Passover—the festival celebrating God's deliverance of Israel from Egypt.

The timing couldn't be more pointed. On the day before Israel's great celebration of rescue, a decree went out ordering their destruction. The feast that remembered how God saved his people from Pharaoh would now be shadowed by a new threat of annihilation.

Would God save them again?

TWO RESPONSES

The chapter ends with a stark contrast: "The couriers went out, spurred on by the king's command, and the edict was issued in the citadel of Susa. The king and Haman sat down to drink, but the city of Susa was bewildered."

The king and Haman sat down to drink. They celebrated. They had just signed the death warrant for an entire people, and they toasted each other over wine.

Meanwhile, the city of Susa was bewildered. The ordinary citizens—Persian and otherwise—were confused and troubled. Even people who weren't Jewish could see that something terrible had just happened. A whole community they lived alongside, worked with, traded with, had suddenly been condemned to die.

This final image captures so much about how evil works in the world. The powerful celebrate while the innocent suffer. Those in charge toast their own cleverness while common people are left bewildered by the cruelty of their leaders.

But this isn't the end of the story. An orphan girl sits on the throne. A loyal cousin watches from the gate. And somewhere behind it all, a God who has not abandoned his people is already working.

WHAT THIS MEANS FOR US

First, injustice is real—but it's not final. Mordecai saved the king's life and got nothing. Haman showed up and got everything. That's unjust, and the author wants us to feel it. But the story doesn't end there. God has a way of turning things around that we can't see from the middle of the story. The overlooked get remembered. The proud get humbled. It just doesn't always happen on our timeline.

Second, small acts of faithfulness matter more than we know. Mordecai's refusal to bow seemed like a minor act of conscience. It looked foolish, even dangerous. But that refusal would eventually expose Haman for who he really was and set in motion the events that saved the Jewish people. When we choose faithfulness over convenience, we rarely know what we're setting in motion.

Third, evil often disguises itself as practical wisdom. Haman didn't pitch his genocide as hatred—he pitched it as good policy. "These people are different. They don't follow our laws. It's not in your best interest to tolerate them." History is full of evil dressed up as reasonable administration. We need discernment to see through the disguise.

Fourth, indifference enables evil. Xerxes wasn't Haman. He didn't hate the Jews. He just didn't care enough to ask questions. His laziness and self-absorption made him a tool in Haman's hands. Sometimes evil advances not because people actively support it but because good people can't be bothered to resist it.

Fifth, God works through what looks like chance. The lots seemed random, but they gave God's people time. The date that Haman thought was lucky turned out to be long enough for everything to change. God is present even in the dice rolls and coincidences of life, working his purposes through what looks like pure chance.

TALKING POINTS

Here are some ideas to reflect on and discuss:

1. **Mordecai saved the king's life but received no reward, while Haman got promoted.** Have you ever experienced something that felt deeply unfair? How do you respond when good deeds go unrecognized?

2. **Mordecai refused to bow to Haman because of his Jewish identity.** When is it right to refuse to go along with what everyone else is doing? How do you know when to take that kind of stand?

3. **Haman wanted to kill all Jews because of one man's actions.** Why do you think hatred often works this way—blaming a whole group for what one person did?

4. **King Xerxes didn't ask questions before approving Haman's plan.** What's dangerous about leaders who don't investigate before making big decisions? What responsibility do followers have to question authority?

5. **The city of Susa was "bewildered" by the decree.** What does this suggest about how ordinary people felt about the planned massacre? What can ordinary people do when their government does something wrong?

The decree has gone out. The date has been set. In eleven months, the Jews will die. But the king doesn't know his own wife is Jewish. And somewhere in the royal chronicles, a forgotten act of loyalty is waiting to be remembered.

Turn the page.

4

FOR SUCH A TIME AS THIS

In *The Lord of the Rings*, there's a moment when Frodo is overwhelmed by the weight of carrying the Ring. He never asked for this burden. He didn't choose to be the one responsible for the fate of Middle-earth. He's just a hobbit—a small, ordinary person from a quiet corner of the world. "I wish the Ring had never come to me," Frodo says to Gandalf. "I wish none of this had happened." Gandalf's response is one of the most famous lines in the story: "So do all who live to see such times. But that is not for them to decide. All we have to decide is what to do with the time that is given us."

That's the question Esther faces in chapter 4. She didn't ask to be queen. She didn't choose to be in the palace when a death sentence was issued against her people. She's in a position she never sought, facing a crisis she never wanted. And now she has to decide what to do with the time that has been given her.

A NATION IN MOURNING

When the decree went out announcing the destruction of the

Jews, the response was immediate and devastating: "When Mordecai learned of all that had been done, he tore his clothes, put on sackcloth and ashes, and went out into the city, wailing loudly and bitterly. But he went only as far as the king's gate, because no one clothed in sackcloth was allowed to enter it. In every province to which the edict and order of the king came, there was great mourning among the Jews, with fasting, weeping and wailing. Many lay in sackcloth and ashes."

Picture the scene. Throughout the vast Persian Empire—from India to Ethiopia—Jewish communities are receiving the news. In eleven months, they will all be killed. Men, women, children. Everyone.

The response is universal grief. Tearing clothes, wearing rough sackcloth, covering themselves with ashes—these were ancient ways of expressing overwhelming sorrow. Mordecai went out into the city wailing. The Hebrew words describe a cry that is loud, bitter, and great—the sound of someone whose heart is breaking.

But notice something: Mordecai went only as far as the king's gate. He couldn't enter because Persian law forbade wearing mourning clothes in that area. Even in his deepest grief, Mordecai respected the rules.

Why would he go to the gate at all? Because that was as close as he could get to Esther. He knew she was in the palace. He needed to reach her. And standing at the gate in sackcloth and ashes was sure to get her attention.

THE QUEEN WHO DIDN'T KNOW

"When Esther's maids and eunuchs came and told her about

Mordecai, she was in great distress. She sent clothes for him to put on instead of his sackcloth, but he would not accept them."

Here's something striking: Esther didn't know what was going on. Every Jew in the empire was mourning, and the queen had no idea why. She was so insulated in the palace, so cut off from her own community, that she hadn't even heard about the decree that condemned her people to death.

Her first response is revealing. When she hears Mordecai is in mourning clothes, she sends him regular clothes. Maybe she's embarrassed by the public display. Maybe she thinks new clothes will fix whatever's wrong. Maybe she just doesn't want to deal with something unpleasant.

It's a very human reaction. When we encounter someone else's pain, our first instinct is often to make it go away—not by addressing the cause, but by covering it up. "Cheer up." "Look on the bright side." "Here, put on something nicer." But Mordecai refuses the clothes. This isn't a problem that can be covered over. This requires action.

"Then Esther summoned Hathach, one of the king's eunuchs assigned to attend her, and ordered him to find out what was troubling Mordecai and why." Finally, Esther asks what's actually going on. What follows is an extended conversation between Esther and Mordecai, conducted entirely through Hathach as their messenger. They can't speak directly—the palace walls separate them. But through this back-and-forth, the stakes become clear.

"Mordecai told him everything that had happened to him, including the exact amount of money Haman had promised to pay into the royal treasury for the destruction of the Jews. He also gave him a copy of the text of the edict for their annihilation, which had been published in Susa, to show to Esther and explain it to her, and he told him to urge her to go into the king's presence to beg for mercy and plead with him for her people."

Mordecai holds nothing back. He tells Esther everything—how Haman manipulated the king, how much money was involved, what the decree actually says. He even sends her a copy of the written edict so she can read the death sentence with her own eyes.

And then comes the challenge: go to the king. Plead for your people.

A DANGEROUS REQUEST

Esther's response shows that she understood immediately how dangerous this would be: "All the king's officials and the people of the royal provinces know that for any man or woman who approaches the king in the inner court without being summoned the king has but one law: that they be put to death. The only exception to this is for the king to extend the gold scepter to them and spare their life. But thirty days have passed since I was called to go to the king."

We need to understand why Esther was so afraid. Persian kings were essentially untouchable. You couldn't just walk up and talk to them. The system was designed to make the king seem like a god—distant, powerful, unapproachable. Guards with axes stood around the throne, ready to execute anyone who entered without permission.

There was exactly one exception: if the king chose to extend his golden scepter, the uninvited visitor would be spared.

But that was entirely up to the king. If he was in a bad mood, if he was busy, if he simply didn't want to be bothered—the intruder would die.

And here's the detail that makes it worse: Esther hadn't been summoned to the king in thirty days. Whatever affection Xerxes once had for her seemed to have cooled. Five years into their marriage, she wasn't exactly his favorite anymore. What made her think he would welcome an uninvited visit?

Esther's fear was completely reasonable. This wasn't paranoia—it was an accurate assessment of the danger. Going to the king uninvited really could get her killed.

MORDECAI'S CHALLENGE

If Esther expected Mordecai to back down once he understood the risk, she was wrong: "Do not think that because you are in the king's house you alone of all the Jews will escape. For if you remain silent at this time, relief and deliverance for the Jews will arise from another place, but you and your father's family will perish."

Mordecai's words are blunt. He tells Esther not to imagine that being queen will protect her. When Haman's men come to kill the Jews, they won't check to see if anyone has a palace address. Esther will die with the rest of her people—unless something changes.

But then Mordecai says something remarkable: "Relief and deliverance for the Jews will arise from another place." Stop and think about what this means. Mordecai is confident—absolutely certain—that the Jewish people will not be destroyed. Even if Esther does nothing, help will come from somewhere.

Deliverance will happen.

How could he be so sure? The text doesn't say directly, but the answer has to be his faith. Mordecai believed in the God of Abraham, Isaac, and Jacob—the God who had made promises to his people that he would not break. God had sworn to preserve the line through which the Messiah would come. That promise couldn't fail, even if Esther failed.

This is one of the clearest hints of God's presence in a book that never names him. Mordecai doesn't say "God will deliver us"—but what else could he mean by "another place"? His confidence comes from somewhere beyond politics and human planning. It comes from trust in divine faithfulness.

But here's the sobering part: just because God will accomplish his purposes doesn't mean Esther gets to sit this one out. If she refuses to act, deliverance will come another way—but she and her family will perish. God's plan will succeed with or without her. The question is whether she'll be part of it.

Then comes the most famous line in the book: "And who knows but that you have come to your royal position for such a time as this?"

SUCH A TIME AS THIS

"For such a time as this." These words have echoed through history. They've challenged countless people to step up in their own difficult moments, to recognize that maybe—just maybe—their circumstances aren't random. Maybe they've been placed where they are for a purpose they're only beginning to understand.

Mordecai isn't making a promise. He says "who knows"—

this is a question, not a statement. He can't be certain why Esther became queen or what God intended by it. But he can see the obvious possibility: all those circumstances that brought Esther to the palace—her beauty, the king's search for a new queen, the favor she kept finding—maybe none of that was coincidence. Maybe it was preparation.

Here's the thing about purpose: we usually can't see it in advance. Joseph didn't know when he was sold into slavery that he would one day save his family from famine. Moses didn't know when he fled Egypt that he would return to deliver his people. David didn't know when he was tending sheep that he was being prepared for kingship.

Looking backward, we can sometimes trace God's hand through our circumstances. Looking forward, we have to step out in faith, trusting that the One who brought us here has a reason.

Mordecai is inviting Esther to trust. You're in the palace. You're the queen. A crisis has arrived that requires exactly what you're positioned to provide. Is that coincidence? Or providence?

The answer would determine everything.

ESTHER'S DECISION

The next verses show Esther transformed: "Then Esther sent this reply to Mordecai: 'Go, gather together all the Jews who are in Susa, and fast for me. Do not eat or drink for three days, night or day. I and my maids will fast as you do. When this is done, I will go to the king, even though it is against the law. And if I perish, I perish.'"

Something has shifted. The woman who sent clothes to make the problem go away is now taking charge. The queen who offered excuses is now giving orders. The girl who hid her identity is about to risk everything for her people.

Notice who's directing whom. At the beginning of chapter 4, Mordecai was telling Esther what to do. By the end, Esther is commanding Mordecai. The chapter traces a reversal—the passive girl becomes an active leader.

Her plan has two parts. First, fasting. She asks all the Jews in Susa to join her in a complete fast—no food or water for three days. This wasn't just skipping meals. It was an intense act of desperation, the kind of thing people did when only divine intervention could help.

The book still doesn't mention prayer directly, but fasting in the Bible is almost always connected to prayer. When people fasted, they were crying out to God. By calling for a fast, Esther was essentially calling for concentrated, united prayer on her behalf.

Second, action. After the fast, she will go to the king. She acknowledges it's against the law. She knows she might die. But she's going anyway. "If I perish, I perish."

These words aren't fatalism—they're faith. Esther isn't saying "whatever happens, happens" with a shrug. She's saying "I've counted the cost, and I'm willing to pay it." She's placing her life in God's hands and moving forward.

The chapter ends simply: "So Mordecai went away and carried out all of Esther's instructions." The man who started by giving orders now follows them. The girl who once obeyed Mordecai in everything now directs him. The hidden Jew is about to reveal herself as a defender of her people.

WHAT THIS MEANS FOR US

First, isolation from God's people is dangerous. Esther was so insulated in the palace that she didn't even know her community was under threat. When we cut ourselves off from other Christians, when we get so comfortable in our own worlds that we lose touch with what's happening to God's people around us and around the world, we become like Esther before the wakeup call. We need connection to see clearly.

Second, covering over problems doesn't solve them. Esther's first instinct was to send clothes—to make the unpleasant situation go away without actually addressing it. But real crises require real engagement. Sometimes the most loving thing we can do is stop trying to fix the surface and start dealing with what's underneath.

Third, God's purposes will succeed—but we can miss our part in them. Mordecai's confidence that deliverance would come "from another place" is comforting and sobering at the same time. God doesn't need us. His plans won't fail just because we refuse to participate. But if we refuse, we lose the privilege of being part of what he's doing. And that loss matters.

Fourth, your circumstances might be preparation. You're where you are for reasons you may not fully understand. The skills you've developed, the relationships you've built, the position you've been placed in—these might be exactly what's needed for a crisis you haven't encountered yet. Live in a way that's ready to respond when the moment comes.

Fifth, faith and action go together. Esther didn't choose between trusting God and doing something. She fasted (an act of dependence on God) and then went to the king (an act of courageous initiative). Real faith doesn't sit back and wait for miracles—it takes the risks that trust makes possible.

TALKING POINTS

Here are some things to reflect on and talk about:

1. **Esther was so isolated in the palace that she didn't know about the crisis facing her people.** How can we stay connected to what's happening in the lives of other Christians, especially those facing hardship?

2. **Mordecai was confident that deliverance would come "from another place" even if Esther didn't act.** What do you think gave him that confidence? How does it change things to know that God's purposes don't depend on us?

3. **"For such a time as this" suggests Esther's circumstances might have been divine preparation.** Can you think of a time when your circumstances seemed to prepare you for something you didn't expect?

4. **Esther called for fasting before she took action.** Why do you think she combined spiritual preparation with practical steps? How do faith and action work together in your life?

5. **Esther said, "If I perish, I perish."** What gave her the courage to risk her life? What would have to be true for you to take that kind of risk?

The fast has begun. Three days without food or water. A queen preparing to break the law. When it ends, Esther will put on her royal robes and walk uninvited into the presence of the most powerful man on earth. Will the king extend his scepter? Or will his guards cut her down?

Turn the page.

5

THE LONG GAME

In *Home Alone*, Kevin McCallister doesn't just hide from the burglars and hope they go away. He makes a plan.

When Harry and Marv announce they're coming to rob his house, Kevin has a choice. He could panic. He could run to the neighbors. He could try to fight two grown men directly—which would be a disaster. Instead, he spends his time preparing. Paint cans on strings. Blowtorches behind doors. Ornaments scattered across the floor. Tar on the stairs. A tarantula in a strategic location.

What makes Kevin's plan work isn't just that he's clever. It's that he thinks ahead. He knows the burglars will come through the front door, so he sets up his first traps there. He knows they'll try the back door next, so he's ready for that too. He leads them exactly where he wants them to go, step by step, until they're defeated by a series of moves they never saw coming.

Chapter 5 of Esther shows us a similar kind of thinking. Esther has decided to risk her life by approaching the king uninvited. But what happens next isn't a desperate plea or an emotional confrontation. It's a carefully planned strategy that will position everyone exactly where they need to be for the confrontation to come.

Esther isn't just brave. She's smart.

THE MOMENT OF TRUTH

"On the third day Esther put on her royal robes and stood in the inner court of the palace, in front of the king's hall. The king was sitting on his royal throne in the hall, facing the entrance."

Three days of fasting are over. Esther has prepared herself spiritually. Now she prepares herself physically—putting on her royal robes, presenting herself not as a frightened petitioner but as the Queen of Persia.

The phrase "put on her royal robes" is actually more than it sounds. In the original language, it literally says she "put on royalty." She clothed herself in her identity. She was going to face the king not as a scared girl hoping for mercy but as his royal counterpart, his queen, someone with legitimate standing in his presence.

Picture the scene. The throne room was massive—archaeologists have found similar rooms at other Persian sites with columns soaring sixty-five feet high. The king sat on his elevated throne, surrounded by guards and officials. Among those guards were soldiers with axes, ready to execute anyone who approached without permission.

Esther stood in the doorway. The king looked up. Everything hung on what happened next. "When he saw Queen Esther standing in the court, he was pleased with her and held out to her the gold scepter that was in his hand. So Esther approached and touched the tip of the scepter."

He extended the scepter. All the tension of chapter 4—the fasting, the fear, the "if I perish, I perish"—resolves in a single gesture. The king was pleased with Esther. He welcomed her. She approached and touched the scepter, completing the ritual that guaranteed her safety.

She lived.

AN UNEXPECTED REQUEST

The king's first question shows he understood something was going on. You don't break protocol and risk death just to say hello. "Then the king asked, 'What is it, Queen Esther? What is your request? Even up to half the kingdom, it will be given you.'"

"Up to half the kingdom" was a traditional expression—ancient royalty's way of saying "I'm feeling generous, ask me for whatever you want." It wasn't meant literally, but it signaled that the king was in a good mood and ready to grant a significant request.

This was Esther's moment. The king was receptive. She had his attention. She could have laid out the whole situation right there—revealed Haman's plot, exposed his lies, begged for her people's lives.

Instead, she did something surprising: "'If it pleases the king,' replied Esther, 'let the king, together with Haman, come today to a banquet I have prepared for him.'" That's it. Come to dinner. Oh, and bring Haman.

Wait—what? Why doesn't she make her real request? Why invite the enemy to a private dinner? Why delay when her people's lives hang in the balance? This is where we see Esther's wisdom. She wasn't just brave—she was strategic.

THE STRATEGY BEHIND THE BANQUET

Think about what Esther was attempting. She needed to convince the king to reverse a decision he had already approved. She needed to expose his most trusted advisor as a villain. She needed to do this without making the king look foolish for trusting Haman in the first place. And she needed to accomplish all of this as a woman in a culture where women had almost no power.

A direct confrontation in the throne room—surrounded by officials and guards, with Haman possibly present—was not the best approach. Too many witnesses. Too much pressure on the king to save face. Too easy for Haman to defend himself or spin the situation.

But a private dinner? That changed everything. By inviting Haman to dine with the royal couple, Esther accomplished several things. First, she created an intimate setting where she could make her case without an audience. Second, she placed Haman in a position where he would be overconfident and off-guard. Third, she gave herself time to read the situation and find the perfect moment.

And there may have been another layer to her strategy. By including Haman in an exclusive invitation—just the king, the queen, and the prime minister—she was subtly planting seeds of jealousy. What husband wants his wife giving special attention to another man? Even if the king didn't consciously realize it, having Haman inserted into their private time might create an undercurrent of irritation.

The king agreed immediately: "'Bring Haman at once,' the king said, 'so that we may do what Esther asks.'"

Notice that last phrase: "so that we may do what Esther asks." Esther is now directing the king's actions. The woman who once passively accepted whatever happened to her is now actively shaping events.

DINNER AND DELAY

"So the king and Haman went to the banquet Esther had prepared. As they were drinking wine, the king again asked Esther, 'Now what is your petition? It will be given you. And what is your request? Even up to half the kingdom, it will be granted.'"

The banquet was pleasant. The wine flowed freely. The king was relaxed and happy. And once again he asked Esther what she really wanted.

Once again, she didn't tell him: "Esther replied, 'My petition and my request is this: If the king regards me with favor and if it pleases the king to grant my petition and fulfill my request, let the king and Haman come tomorrow to the banquet I will prepare for them. Then I will answer the king's question.'"

Another banquet. Another delay. Tomorrow she'll explain.

This must have been agonizing. Every hour that passed was another hour closer to the day when all Jews would be killed. Esther had the king's attention, his favor, his promise to grant her request. Why not press forward?

We can only guess at her reasons. Maybe she sensed the timing wasn't quite right. Maybe she wanted Haman even more relaxed and confident before she exposed him. Maybe God was guiding her to wait for circumstances that hadn't fallen into place yet.

The book doesn't explain Esther's thinking. It simply shows

her acting with patience and precision, playing a long game when everything in her must have wanted to rush.

Whatever her reasons, the delay would prove crucial. Events were about to unfold overnight that would make tomorrow's banquet far more powerful than today's could have been.

HAMAN'S DANGEROUS JOY

The scene now shifts to Haman: "Haman went out that day happy and in high spirits." Think about what just happened from Haman's perspective. He was invited to an exclusive dinner with the king and queen—just the three of them. No other officials. No other nobles. Just Haman. And he's been invited back tomorrow for another one.

He must have felt like the most important man in the world. His influence was so great that even the queen wanted his company. His position was unassailable. His future was golden.

Then he walked past the king's gate: "But when he saw Mordecai at the king's gate and observed that he neither rose nor showed fear in his presence, he was filled with rage against Mordecai."

There was Mordecai. Still sitting there. Still refusing to bow. Still showing no fear of the most powerful official in the empire.

Haman's mood crashed instantly. All the joy of the banquet, all the honor of the exclusive invitation—none of it mattered because one man wouldn't bow to him.

This reveals something important about Haman's character. His happiness was completely dependent on everyone treating him with the respect he thought he deserved. One person's refusal to comply was enough to poison everything else. A thousand honors meant nothing if there was one holdout.

This is the nature of pride. It can never be satisfied. There's always someone who isn't impressed, some recognition that's missing, some slight that spoils everything. Pride is a hunger that feeding only makes worse.

"Nevertheless, Haman restrained himself and went home." For now, he controlled his anger. But it was building.

BOASTING AND BITTERNESS

"Calling together his friends and Zeresh, his wife, Haman boasted to them about his vast wealth, his many sons, and all the ways the king had honored him and how he had elevated him above the other nobles and officials."

Haman gathered an audience and started listing his accomplishments. His wealth. His ten sons. His promotions. His status above every other official in the kingdom.

And then the cherry on top: "'And that's not all,' Haman added. 'I'm the only person Queen Esther invited to accompany the king to the banquet she gave. And she has invited me along with the king tomorrow.'"

He's savoring every detail. He's the most important man in Persia. The queen herself recognizes it. Tomorrow he'll dine with royalty again.

But then his mood darkened: "But all this gives me no satisfaction as long as I see that Jew Mordecai sitting at the king's gate."

Read that again. "All this gives me no satisfaction." His vast wealth—worthless. His many sons—meaningless. His unprecedented power—empty. The queen's exclusive invitation—hollow.

One man's refusal to bow has ruined everything.

This is one of the saddest statements in the entire book. Haman had more than almost anyone could dream of. Yet he experienced none of the joy it should have brought. His obsession with Mordecai had consumed him so completely that nothing else could make him happy.

The book of Proverbs says "a heart at peace gives life to the body, but envy rots the bones" (14:30). Haman's bones were rotting. His hatred was eating him alive.

A DEADLY SUGGESTION

Haman's wife and friends had a solution: "His wife Zeresh and all his friends said to him, 'Have a pole set up, reaching to a height of seventy-five feet, and ask the king in the morning to have Mordecai impaled on it. Then go with the king to the banquet and enjoy yourself.'"

The suggestion is breathtaking in its casual cruelty. The answer to Haman's unhappiness, according to his wife, was simple: crucify the man who bothered him. Then he could enjoy his dinner party.

The crucifixion pole was to be seventy-five feet tall. That's absurdly high—about as tall as a seven-story building. Why so tall? To make a public spectacle. To humiliate Mordecai in death. To demonstrate Haman's power in the most visible way possible.

"This suggestion delighted Haman, and he had the pole set up." He didn't hesitate. He didn't consider whether this was just. He didn't worry about executing an innocent man. He simply ordered the construction to begin immediately.

As chapter 5 ends, we're left in suspense. Esther has positioned herself for tomorrow's banquet, but she doesn't know about the pole being built tonight. Haman plans to ask the king for Mordecai's death first thing in the morning—before the banquet even happens.

From a human perspective, Esther's careful strategy might fail. Mordecai could be dead before she ever makes her request. Her wisdom might be undone by Haman's hatred.

But there's still the night ahead. And in that night, something is about to happen that neither Esther nor Haman nor anyone else could have planned.

WHAT THIS MEANS FOR US

First, courage and wisdom go together. Esther didn't just barge in and blurt out her request. She combined bravery with strategy, timing her approach for maximum effect. Sometimes the most courageous thing is to wait, to think, to plan—not because we're afraid, but because we want our courage to actually accomplish something.

Second, pride can never be satisfied. Haman had everything—wealth, power, family, honor—and none of it was enough because one man wouldn't bow. Pride is a trap. The more you feed it, the hungrier it gets. The more recognition you receive, the more you need. True contentment doesn't come from having everyone's respect. It comes from something deeper.

Third, hatred destroys the hater. Mordecai wasn't suffering because Haman was angry at him. Mordecai was just sitting at the gate, doing his job. Haman was the one whose joy was poisoned, whose peace was stolen, whose mind was consumed. Bitterness and unforgiveness hurt us more than they hurt the people we resent.

Fourth, God works through our wisdom and beyond it. Esther planned carefully, but she couldn't have planned what was about to happen overnight. She did her part; God would do his. Our responsibility is to act with wisdom and faith. God's work often goes beyond anything we could strategize or anticipate.

Fifth, the tables can turn faster than we expect. Haman went to bed that night confident he was about to destroy his enemy and enjoy the queen's banquet. He had no idea how completely his world was about to collapse. Sometimes the proudest moments come right before the greatest falls.

TALKING POINTS

Here are some questions to consider and discuss:

1. **Esther delayed making her request even when the king seemed ready to grant it.** When might patience and timing be more important than immediate action? Can you think of a situation where waiting made something work out better?

2. **Haman said that all his wealth, power, and honor gave him "no satisfaction" because of Mordecai's refusal to bow.** Why do you think he couldn't just ignore Mordecai and enjoy what he had? What does this teach us about pride?

3. **Zeresh suggested killing Mordecai so Haman could "enjoy himself" at the banquet.** What does this reveal about how Haman's family and friends thought about human life? How does this contrast with how God views people?

4. **Esther combined spiritual preparation (fasting) with practical wisdom (strategic timing).** How do faith and wisdom work together in your own life? Do you tend toward one more than the other?

5. **At the end of chapter 5, both Esther and Haman have plans for tomorrow.** Neither knows what the other is doing. What does this tell us about how limited our perspective is and how much we need to trust God?

Two banquets are planned. A seventy-five-foot pole is being built. Mordecai's life hangs by a thread. But tonight, the king won't be able to sleep. And that sleepless night will change everything.

Turn the page.

6

THE NIGHT EVERYTHING CHANGED

You know that feeling when you're playing a board game and everything seems to be going against you? Your opponent has all the best properties, all the money, all the luck. Every roll of the dice makes things worse for you. You're pretty sure you're about to lose.

And then something completely unexpected happens. Your opponent lands on your one hotel. Or draws a card that changes everything. Or makes a terrible mistake they can't take back. Suddenly the whole game flips, and you go from losing to winning in a way nobody could have predicted.

In the game of *Uno*, there's a card called "Reverse." When someone plays it, the direction of play changes instantly. The person who thought they were about to win suddenly finds themselves on the defensive. Everything that was working in their favor now works against them.

Chapter 6 of Esther is the ultimate reverse card. It's the night when everything changes—not because of any dramatic action by the main characters, but because of something as simple as a king who couldn't fall asleep.

A SLEEPLESS NIGHT

"That night the king could not sleep." That's it. That's the sentence that changes everything. Think about what's happening at this moment in the story. Haman has built a seventy-five-foot pole to crucify Mordecai. He plans to ask the king for permission first thing in the morning. By breakfast time, Mordecai should be dead. Esther has no idea this is coming—she's planning her second banquet, thinking she has time.

From a human perspective, the situation looks hopeless. Even if Esther's plan works perfectly, it will be too late. Mordecai will already be dead by the time she makes her request.

But that night, the king couldn't sleep. The text doesn't tell us why. He wasn't having bad dreams. He wasn't worried about anything in particular. Sleep just wouldn't come. It's the most ordinary thing in the world—everyone has nights like that sometimes.

But this ordinary, unexplained event is the hinge on which the entire story turns. This is where we see God's fingerprints most clearly in a book that never mentions his name. The ancient Greek translation of Esther actually adds a phrase here: "The Lord took sleep from the king that night." The translators wanted to make explicit what the original author left implicit.

God was at work in the most ordinary way imaginable.

BEDTIME READING

What do you do when you can't sleep? Watch TV? Read a book? Scroll through your phone? King Xerxes had his servants read to him: "So he ordered the book of the chronicles, the record of his reign, to be brought in and read to him."

The "book of the chronicles" was the official record of everything that happened during the king's reign—a detailed log of court business, important events, rewards given, and services rendered. It was basically the most boring reading material in the palace. Maybe Xerxes thought it would put him to sleep.

Instead, the reader came to a particular entry: "It was found recorded there that Mordecai had exposed Bigthana and Teresh, two of the king's officers who guarded the doorway, who had conspired to assassinate King Xerxes."

Remember this? Way back in chapter 2, Mordecai had uncovered a plot to kill the king. He reported it through Esther. The conspirators were executed. The event was recorded in the official chronicle.

And then … nothing. Mordecai was supposed to receive a reward. Persian kings were famous for generously honoring people who helped them—it was good for their reputation and encouraged future loyalty. But somehow, Mordecai's reward never happened. For five years, this oversight sat in the records, unnoticed and uncorrected.

Until tonight. "'What honor and recognition has Mordecai received for this?' the king asked. 'Nothing has been done for him,' his attendants answered." The king was bothered. This was embarrassing. A man saves the king's life, and the king forgets to reward him? That makes the king look bad. This needed to be fixed immediately.

PERFECT TIMING

"The king said, 'Who is in the court?'" The king wanted advice.

Who could he consult at this hour about how to properly honor someone?

As it happened, someone was there: "Now Haman had just entered the outer court of the palace to speak to the king about impaling Mordecai on the pole he had set up for him."

Let that sink in. Haman had arrived at the palace in the early morning darkness, eager to be first in line to see the king. He couldn't wait to request Mordecai's execution. He was so excited about watching his enemy die that he'd probably barely slept himself.

And at the exact moment when Haman arrived to ask for Mordecai's death, the king was looking for someone to advise him on Mordecai's reward.

The timing is almost comically perfect. If Haman had arrived five minutes earlier, he might have gotten his request in before the king started thinking about rewards. If the reader had chosen a different section of the chronicles, Mordecai's story might never have come up. If the king had been able to sleep, none of this would have happened. But it all lined up exactly this way—at exactly this moment. Coincidence? The author wants us to wonder.

"His attendants answered, 'Haman is standing in the court.' 'Bring him in,' the king ordered." Haman walked in, probably rehearsing his speech about why Mordecai needed to die. He had no idea what he was walking into.

THE QUESTION

"When Haman entered, the king asked him, 'What should be done for the man the king delights to honor?'" Put yourself in Haman's shoes. You've just walked in, and the king immediately asks how he should honor someone. No context. No explanation. Just: "What should be done for the man the king delights to honor?"

Who would the king want to honor? Haman's mind raced through the possibilities. And his pride landed on the obvious answer: "Now Haman thought to himself, 'Who is there that the king would rather honor than me?'"

Of course. It had to be him. He was the king's favorite. He'd just been invited to two exclusive dinners with the royal couple. Who else could the king possibly want to honor this much?

Haman didn't ask who the king had in mind. He didn't pause to gather information. He was so certain the honor was meant for himself that he launched straight into describing the most extravagant reward he could imagine: "So he answered the king, 'For the man the king delights to honor, have them bring a royal robe the king has worn and a horse the king has ridden, one with a royal crest placed on its head. Then let the robe and horse be entrusted to one of the king's most noble princes. Let them robe the man the king delights to honor, and lead him on the horse through the city streets, proclaiming before him, "This is what is done for the man the king delights to honor!"'"

Notice what Haman asks for. Not money—he already had plenty. Not land or titles—he already had the highest position in the kingdom. He wanted to be treated like the king himself. He wanted to wear the king's clothes, ride the king's horse, be paraded through the streets while a nobleman announced his greatness to everyone.

This was Haman's fantasy. This was what he dreamed about when no one was watching. And now the king was asking him to describe it out loud. What Haman didn't know was that every word he spoke was building the trap that would spring on himself.

THE REVERSAL

The king loved it. "'Go at once,' the king commanded Haman. 'Get the robe and the horse and do just as you have suggested for Mordecai the Jew, who sits at the king's gate. Do not neglect anything you have recommended.'"

Imagine the moment those words landed. Haman had walked in expecting to request Mordecai's death. Instead, he's ordered to give Mordecai the highest public honor in the kingdom—an honor he had designed for himself, described in his own words.

"Do not neglect anything you have recommended." Everything Haman had suggested. The royal robe. The royal horse. The parade through the streets. The public announcement. And Haman himself—"one of the king's most noble princes"—would have to be the one leading the horse and making the proclamation.

The text doesn't describe Haman's reaction. It doesn't need to. We can imagine the blood draining from his face, the words catching in his throat, the world spinning as he realized what had just happened. He had come to destroy Mordecai. Now he had to honor him.

THE PARADE

"So Haman got the robe and the horse. He robed Mordecai,

and led him on horseback through the city streets, proclaiming before him, 'This is what is done for the man the king delights to honor!'"

Picture this scene. Mordecai—the man who refused to bow to Haman—is now dressed in the king's own robe, sitting on the king's own horse. And Haman—the second most powerful man in the empire—is walking in front of him like a servant, announcing to everyone that the king delights to honor this man.

Every person watching knew who Haman was. Everyone knew about his feud with Mordecai. Everyone could see the humiliation on Haman's face as he spoke words he never wanted to say about a man he wanted to kill.

Mordecai, meanwhile, remains remarkably passive through all of this. He doesn't gloat. He doesn't say anything to Haman. He simply accepts the honor and then goes back to his normal place at the king's gate: "Afterward Mordecai returned to the king's gate."

Mordecai seems to understand that this honor, while wonderful, doesn't actually change anything about the bigger situation. His people are still under a death sentence. The parade doesn't fix that. So he goes back to waiting—and probably praying—for deliverance.

HAMAN'S COLLAPSE

"But Haman rushed home, with his head covered in grief, and told Zeresh his wife and all his friends everything that had happened to him." The covering of the head was a sign of mourning and shame. Haman, who had gone out that morning expecting triumph, came home devastated. He had been publicly humiliated in front of the entire city. The man he hated most in the world had been honored while Haman walked in the dust beside him.

He poured out the whole story to his wife and advisors—the same people who had told him the day before to build the pole and impale Mordecai on it.

Their response was not comforting: "His advisers and his wife Zeresh said to him, 'Since Mordecai, before whom your downfall has started, is of Jewish origin, you cannot stand against him—you will surely come to ruin!'"

Wait—weren't these the same people who encouraged Haman's plan against Mordecai? Now suddenly they're warning him that he can't win?

Something has shifted. Haman's advisors have seen the writing on the wall. Somehow, even these pagans recognize that there's something special about the Jewish people. They've survived everything—exile, conquest, displacement—and they keep surviving. There's a power behind them that Haman can't overcome.

"You will surely come to ruin." The very people who supported Haman's rise are now predicting his fall. The reversal is complete—and Haman knows it.

NO TIME TO PROCESS

"While they were still talking with him, the king's eunuchs arrived and hurried Haman away to the banquet Esther had prepared." Haman doesn't even have time to absorb what's happening. Officials show up to escort him to Esther's second dinner party. Remember that second banquet he was so excited about yesterday? The one he bragged about to his wife and friends?

Now he has to go sit through a meal with the king and queen while his world is collapsing around him. The word "hurried" suggests urgency, even force. Haman is being rushed from one disaster toward another. He's lost control of everything. Events are moving faster than he can react. The chapter ends with Haman being swept toward his fate—a fate that will be sealed before the evening is over.

WHAT THIS MEANS FOR US

First, God works through ordinary events. The king couldn't sleep. The reader happened to pick up a certain section of the chronicle. Haman happened to arrive at just the right moment. None of these things are miraculous. They're completely ordinary. But strung together, they accomplish exactly what needed to happen. God doesn't always work through dramatic supernatural interventions. More often, he works through everyday circumstances—timing, "coincidences," small decisions—that we only recognize as his hand when we look back.

Second, pride sets its own trap. Haman designed his own humiliation. Every detail of Mordecai's honor came from Haman's own mouth—the robe, the horse, the parade, the proclamation. His pride made him assume the honor was for himself, and that assumption became his downfall. When we're convinced we deserve recognition, we often set ourselves up for embarrassment.

Third, God's timing is not our timing. For five years, Mordecai went unrewarded. From a human perspective, the oversight seemed like injustice. But God was saving that recognition for exactly the right moment—the moment when it would not only reward Mordecai but also expose Haman and begin the reversal of the whole situation. What looks like God forgetting may actually be God waiting.

Fourth, the proud will fall. Haman's wife and friends saw it coming before he did. Something about Mordecai's identity as a Jew meant Haman couldn't win against him. The same pattern runs throughout Scripture: those who oppose God's people ultimately oppose God himself, and that's a fight no one wins.

Fifth, small hinges swing big doors. One sleepless night changed everything. One reading from an old record. One mistaken assumption. The entire story pivoted on events that seemed trivial in themselves. Never underestimate how God might use the small, ordinary moments of your life for purposes you can't yet see.

TALKING POINTS

Here are some points to consider and unpack together:

1. **The king's sleepless night seems like a random event, but it changed everything.** Can you think of small, seemingly random events in your own life that turned out to be significant? How might God work through ordinary circumstances?

2. **Haman was so convinced he deserved honor that he never asked who the king wanted to reward.** How does pride blind us to reality? What are ways we can guard against this kind of self-deception?

3. **Mordecai waited five years for recognition that never came—until the exact night it was needed most.** How do

you handle situations where something seems unfair or your efforts go unrecognized? What does this chapter teach about God's timing?

4. **Haman's wife and friends went from encouraging his plan to predicting his ruin.** What does this tell us about the kind of advice we get from people who only tell us what we want to hear?

5. **The chapter ends with Haman being "hurried" to a banquet he can no longer enjoy.** Have you ever experienced something you were looking forward to becoming something you dreaded? How did you handle it?

The man who came to request an execution leaves having announced an honor. The man who expected to be celebrated discovers he's beginning to fall. And a banquet is waiting that will seal everyone's fate.

Turn the page.

7

THE VILLAIN UNMASKED

In almost every superhero story, there's a moment when the villain is finally exposed. Think of *Spider-Man: Homecoming*, when Peter Parker realizes that Adrian Toomes—the Vulture—is actually his date's father. Or *The Incredibles*, when Syndrome's true identity as the rejected kid Buddy is revealed. Or the classic scene in *Scooby-Doo* when the gang pulls off the mask and everyone gasps, "Old Man Jenkins?!"

These unmasking moments are satisfying because we've been waiting for them. We've watched the villain scheme and plot and hurt people while pretending to be trustworthy. We've wanted someone to see through the disguise. And when the truth finally comes out, there's a sense of justice—finally, everyone can see what we've known all along.

Chapter 7 of Esther is the unmasking scene. After all the buildup—the banquets, the delays, the careful planning—Esther finally points her finger at the villain and says his name out loud.

But this unmasking has higher stakes than any superhero movie. Real lives hang in the balance. And the scene moves so fast that by the time it's over, you'll barely have time to catch your breath.

THE SECOND BANQUET

"So the king and Haman went to dine with Queen Esther, and as they were drinking wine on that second day, the king again asked, 'Queen Esther, what is your petition? It will be given you. What is your request? Even up to half the kingdom, it will be granted.'"

Picture the scene. The king arrives, probably still confused about everything that happened the night before—his sleepless reading session, the discovery that Mordecai was never rewarded, the strange scene of Haman leading Mordecai through the streets on a royal horse.

And Haman arrives too, but he's a different man than he was yesterday. Yesterday he was confident, excited, boasting to his friends about his exclusive invitation. Today he's shaken. His wife and advisors have just told him he's doomed. He's been publicly humiliated. And he's been rushed here by the king's servants before he even had time to process what happened.

The banquet begins. Wine is served. And for the third time, the king asks Esther what she really wants. "Even up to half the kingdom," he says again.

This is the moment Esther has been waiting for. She has maneuvered the king into promising—three times now—to grant her request. She has positioned Haman right where she wants him. There's no more delaying.

It's time to speak.

ESTHER'S PLEA

"Then Queen Esther answered, 'If I have found favor with you, O king, and if it pleases your majesty, grant me my life—this is my petition. And spare my people—this is my request.'"

Notice how Esther frames her request. She doesn't start by accusing Haman. She doesn't explain the political background or the history of the decree. She makes it personal. "Grant me my life."

The king must have been stunned. What does she mean, grant her life? Who is threatening the queen? What kind of danger could she possibly be in?

"And spare my people." Now the king learns something he never knew: Esther has a people. She belongs to a group. She has an identity beyond being his queen. But which people? And why do they need to be spared?

Esther continues: "For I and my people have been sold for destruction and slaughter and annihilation. If we had merely been sold as male and female slaves, I would have kept quiet, because no such distress would justify disturbing the king."

The words "destruction and slaughter and annihilation" aren't random. They're the exact words from Haman's decree back in chapter 3. Esther is quoting the death sentence against her people directly to the king's face.

But notice her cleverness. She says "we have been sold"—using the passive voice. She doesn't immediately say who did the selling. She's building suspense, letting the king's anger rise before she names the villain.

And she adds a final twist: if this were merely about slavery, she wouldn't have bothered the king. But this is about extermination. Total destruction. That's worth disturbing even the most powerful man in the world.

THE KING'S QUESTION

The king's response shows that he genuinely had no idea what was going on: "King Xerxes asked Queen Esther, 'Who is he? Where is the man who has dared to do such a thing?'"

Think about what this reveals. The king signed the decree. He gave Haman his signet ring. He authorized the whole thing. But apparently it made so little impression on him that when Esther quotes the exact words of the edict, he doesn't even recognize them. This is a king who didn't ask questions when his prime minister requested permission to destroy an entire ethnic group. He didn't investigate. He didn't check the details. He just handed over his ring and went back to drinking with Haman.

Now he's outraged—not because he suddenly cares about justice, but because someone has threatened his queen. His queen. That makes it personal for him.

"Who is he? Where is the man?" The king wants a name. And Esther is ready to give him one.

THE ACCUSATION

"Esther said, 'The adversary and enemy is this vile Haman!'" There it is. The unmasking. The finger pointed. The name spoken aloud. In one short sentence, Esther identifies Haman three ways: adversary, enemy, vile. She piles up the accusations before even saying his name, letting the weight of the words land before the final blow.

"This vile Haman!"

Imagine Haman's face at this moment. He came to the banquet already shaken from his public humiliation. He sat through the meal knowing his wife and friends predicted his ruin. And now the queen—the woman whose dinner invitation he bragged about yesterday—is pointing at him and calling him an enemy. "Then Haman was terrified before the king and queen."

Of course he was. He had spent months plotting the destruction of the Jewish people. He had manipulated the king into signing the decree. He had built a seventy-five-foot pole to crucify Mordecai. And now, suddenly, the queen reveals that she herself is one of the people he planned to destroy.

Everything is crashing down at once. The queen is Jewish. The man he just publicly honored is her relative. His entire scheme has put him in direct conflict with the king's own wife. Terror is the only reasonable response.

THE KING'S RAGE

"The king got up in a rage, left his wine and went out into the palace garden." The king is furious. But notice what he does with his fury: he walks away. He goes to the garden.

This seems like a strange reaction. Shouldn't he immediately condemn Haman? Order his arrest? Do something?

But the king has a problem. He authorized the decree. He accepted the money (or at least didn't refuse it clearly). If he punishes Haman for the plot, doesn't that implicate himself? How does a king admit he was manipulated by his own advisor without looking foolish?

So Xerxes does what he often does when faced with a difficult decision: he leaves the room to think. He needs a moment to figure out how to handle this without making himself look bad.

Meanwhile, Haman is left alone with the queen—the woman whose people he tried to exterminate.

HAMAN'S DESPERATE PLEA

"But Haman, realizing that the king had already decided his fate, stayed behind to beg Queen Esther for his life." Haman knew the king well. He had watched Xerxes make impulsive decisions before. He had seen how quickly the king's moods could turn deadly. And in the king's rage-filled exit, Haman could read his own death sentence. His only hope was Esther.

Think about the irony. Haman had plotted to destroy every Jew in the empire. Now he's begging a Jewish woman to save him. He wanted Mordecai dead for refusing to bow to him. Now Haman himself is probably on his knees, pleading for mercy from Mordecai's cousin. The man who showed no mercy is now desperate for mercy.

The text doesn't tell us what Esther said—or if she said anything at all. Her silence speaks volumes. Why would she help the man who tried to kill her entire people?

THE FINAL MISTAKE

"Just as the king returned from the palace garden to the banquet hall, Haman was falling on the couch where Esther was reclining." In ancient Persia, people didn't sit at tables to eat formal meals. They reclined on couches. When you wanted to beg someone for mercy, you fell at their feet—which, when they were reclining, meant falling toward the couch they were lying on.

Haman was following the normal custom for pleading. He was throwing himself at Esther's feet, begging for his life. But the king didn't see a man begging. He saw something else entirely: "The king exclaimed, 'Will he even molest the queen while she is with me in the house?'"

The king interpreted Haman's desperate gesture as an attack on Esther. Whether Xerxes genuinely misunderstood or simply chose to interpret it that way (which would solve his problem of how to punish Haman without admitting his own role in the decree), the result was the same. In the king's eyes, Haman had just committed the ultimate offense: assaulting the queen in the king's own house.

"As soon as the word left the king's mouth, they covered Haman's face." When servants covered a person's face, it meant they were already condemned. It was like putting a hood over someone about to be executed. Haman wasn't just in trouble anymore—he was a dead man.

HAMAN'S DEATH

"Then Harbona, one of the eunuchs attending the king, said, 'A pole seventy-five feet high stands by Haman's house. He had it made for Mordecai, who spoke up to help the king.'"

Someone in the palace had been paying attention. Harbona knew about the pole Haman built. He knew it was intended for Mordecai—the same Mordecai who had saved the king's life by exposing the assassination plot.

This detail sealed Haman's fate. Not only had he plotted

against the queen's people, not only had he (apparently) assaulted the queen herself, but he had also planned to execute the king's benefactor—the man the king had just honored with a parade through the city.

Everything Haman had done was now piled up against him. "The king said, 'Hang him on it!'"

The order was immediate. No trial. No defense. No appeal. The pole Haman built for Mordecai would be used for Haman instead. "So they hanged Haman on the pole he had prepared for Mordecai. Then the king's fury subsided."

The villain who set a trap fell into his own trap. The man who dug a pit for his enemy fell into it himself. The weapon he prepared for Mordecai became the weapon of his own destruction.

There's an old proverb that says "whoever digs a pit will fall into it." Haman is the perfect illustration. His pride, his hatred, his schemes—they all came back on his own head.

WHAT THIS MEANS FOR US

First, hidden truth eventually comes to light. Esther hid her identity for years, but the moment came when she had to reveal it. Haman hid his murderous intentions behind political language, but the moment came when he was exposed. We can hide things for a while, but eventually the truth surfaces. The question is whether we'll be on the right side of truth when it does.

Second, evil destroys itself. Haman wasn't brought down by some outside force. He was brought down by his own actions—his own pride, his own hatred, his own crucifixion pole.

Sin has a way of doing this. The very things we build to hurt others often become the things that hurt us.

Third, the timing of justice isn't always ours to control. Esther had to wait. She had to trust that the right moment would come. And when it came, events moved faster than anyone could have predicted. Sometimes we want justice immediately, but God's timing is often different from ours—and usually better.

Fourth, those who show no mercy often find none. Haman wanted to destroy an entire race of people. When his moment of judgment came, there was no one to speak for him. The mercy he never extended was not extended to him. Jesus said, "Blessed are the merciful, for they will be shown mercy" (Matthew 5:7). The reverse is also true.

Fifth, identity matters. Esther's Jewish identity, hidden for so long, became the most important fact in the room. Who we are—and whose we are—matters more than position or power. When the crisis came, Esther stood with her people, and that identification saved them all.

TALKING POINTS

Here are some thoughts to guide your reflection and discussion:

1. **Esther had hidden her Jewish identity for years before finally revealing it.** Are there parts of your identity or faith that you tend to hide? What would it take for you to "come out" about them?

2. **The king was furious when he learned his queen was threatened, but he himself had authorized the decree.** How do people sometimes get angry about problems they helped

create? How can we recognize when we're doing this ourselves?

3. **Haman begged for mercy from the very person whose people he tried to destroy.** What does this tell us about how desperate situations can change people—at least temporarily? Do you think Haman was truly sorry or just afraid?

4. **Haman was executed on the pole he built for someone else.** Can you think of other examples—from history, from stories, or from life—where someone's plan to hurt others backfired on them?

5. **At the end of chapter 7, Haman is dead, but the decree against the Jews is still in effect.** What does this teach us about how solving one problem doesn't always solve every problem?

The villain is dead. The king's anger has subsided. But the decree remains. The death sentence against the Jewish people is still written in the law of the Medes and Persians—a law that cannot be changed. Haman's execution is only the beginning of the solution, not the end.

Turn the page.

8

THE PROBLEM THAT WON'T GO AWAY

You know those movies where the heroes defeat the villain, everyone cheers, and then … the movie keeps going? Because it turns out defeating the villain didn't actually solve the problem.

In *Avengers: Infinity War*, the heroes fight Thanos with everything they have. But even when they come close to defeating him, they realize that stopping him isn't enough—they need to undo what he's already done. The snap has happened. Half the universe is gone. Beating Thanos doesn't bring anyone back.

Or think about disaster movies where the characters stop the bad guy who activated the bomb, but the bomb is still ticking. The villain is in handcuffs, but the countdown hasn't stopped. They still have to figure out how to defuse it before everything explodes.

That's exactly the situation in Esther 8. Haman is dead. The villain has been defeated. Justice has been served. But the bomb he planted is still ticking.

The decree to destroy all Jews throughout the Persian Empire is still in effect. It's written in the law of the Medes and Persians—law that cannot be changed, cannot be revoked, cannot be undone. And in less than nine months, that decree will be carried out.

Killing Haman was necessary. But it wasn't enough.

REWARDS AND REVERSALS

The chapter begins with some immediate good news: "That same day King Xerxes gave Queen Esther the estate of Haman, the enemy of the Jews. And Mordecai came into the presence of the king, for Esther had told how he was related to her. The king took off his signet ring, which he had reclaimed from Haman, and presented it to Mordecai. And Esther appointed him over Haman's estate."

In a single day, everything flips for Mordecai. The man who had been condemned to death on a seventy-five-foot pole now receives the dead man's entire estate. The Jewish official who sat faithfully at the king's gate now wears the king's signet ring—the same ring that Haman used to seal the death decree.

Think about that ring for a moment. It's the same physical object. But in Haman's hand, it signed death warrants. In Mordecai's hand, it will sign a very different kind of document.

And Esther finally reveals what she's hidden for years: her relationship to Mordecai. She tells the king that this man is her family, her guardian, the one who raised her. The king, who just honored Mordecai with a parade and now learns he's related to his queen, promotes him to the highest position in the kingdom—the position Haman used to hold.

The reversal is complete. Mordecai now has Haman's job, Haman's ring, and Haman's house.

But the decree is still ticking.

THE UNSOLVABLE PROBLEM

Esther understood that defeating Haman was only half the battle: "Esther again pleaded with the king, falling at his feet and weeping. She begged him to put an end to the evil plan of Haman the Agagite, which he had devised against the Jews. Then the king extended the gold scepter to Esther and she arose and stood before him."

Notice that Esther has to approach the king again—and once again she falls at his feet. Even after everything that's happened, even after Haman's execution, even after Mordecai's promotion, she can't assume the king will listen. She has to take the risk again, pleading with tears for her people's lives.

Her request is direct: "'If it pleases the king,' she said, 'and if he regards me with favor and thinks it the right thing to do, and if he is pleased with me, let an order be written overruling the dispatches that Haman son of Hammedatha, the Agagite, devised and wrote to destroy the Jews in all the king's provinces. For how can I bear to see disaster fall on my people? How can I bear to see the destruction of my family?'"

Esther loads her request with layers of "if"—if it pleases you, if you regard me with favor, if it seems right, if you are pleased with me. She's being incredibly careful. She's asking for something that may be impossible.

And the king's response reveals the problem: "King Xerxes replied to Queen Esther and to Mordecai the Jew, 'Because Haman attacked the Jews, I have given his estate to Esther, and they have hanged him on the gallows. Now write another decree in the king's name in behalf of the Jews as seems best to you, and seal it with the king's signet ring—for no document written in the king's name and sealed with his ring can be revoked.'"

Do you see what the king is saying? He can't undo Haman's decree. It's impossible. Once a law has been written in the king's name and sealed with his ring, it cannot be revoked. The Persian legal system had no mechanism for changing its own laws.

This sounds absurd to us. What kind of government can't change its own laws? But this was actually a point of pride for the Persians. They believed it made their laws more trustworthy. If even the king couldn't change a law, then everyone knew exactly what to expect.

The problem, of course, is that this system assumed the laws would always be just. It had no way to deal with a situation like this, where an evil man manipulated the system to create an evil law.

The death decree cannot be undone. But maybe it can be countered.

A SECOND DECREE

The king's solution is creative: he can't revoke the first decree, but Esther and Mordecai can write a second one. Whatever they come up with, he'll authorize it. "At once the royal secretaries were summoned—on the twenty-third day of the third month, the month of Sivan. They wrote out all Mordecai's orders to the Jews, and to the satraps, governors and nobles of the 127 provinces stretching from India to Cush."

Notice the details. Mordecai's decree follows the exact same process Haman used. Same secretaries. Same officials receiving the message. Same translation into every language of every province. Same seal with the king's ring. Same courier system.

But the content is completely different: "The king's edict granted the Jews in every city the right to assemble and protect themselves; to destroy, kill and annihilate any armed force of any nationality or province that might attack them and their women and children; and to plunder the property of their enemies. The day appointed for the Jews to do this in all the provinces of King Xerxes was the thirteenth day of the twelfth month, the month of Adar."

Let's be clear about what this decree does and doesn't say. It doesn't give the Jews permission to attack anyone they want. It gives them the right to defend themselves against anyone who attacks them. The language is specifically about "any armed force … that might attack them."

Haman's decree had authorized anyone in the empire to attack the Jews. Now Mordecai's decree authorizes the Jews to fight back. The first decree told the attackers they could kill Jews without consequence. The second decree tells the attackers that there will be consequences—the Jews are allowed to defend themselves.

This changes everything. Under Haman's decree alone, attacking Jews would have been risk-free—the government was on your side. Now, anyone who wants to attack the Jews has to consider that the Jews are legally permitted to fight back, and the new prime minister is Jewish.

The decree doesn't eliminate the danger. But it levels the playing field.

THE SAME DATE

Both decrees apply to the same day: the thirteenth of Adar, about nine months away.

Why couldn't Mordecai's decree take effect immediately? Because it had to match Haman's decree. The original decree said the attack on the Jews would happen on that specific day. If Mordecai had authorized Jewish self-defense on a different day, it wouldn't have helped—the Jews still would have been forbidden from defending themselves on the actual day of the attack.

So now the empire has two laws, both applying to the same day: Law One (Haman's): The people of the empire may attack the Jews and take their property. Law Two (Mordecai's): The Jews may defend themselves against anyone who attacks them.

Neither law cancels the other. Both are in effect. The thirteenth of Adar will be a day of confrontation—a day when everyone has to choose which side they're on.

THE FASTEST HORSES

"The couriers, riding the royal horses, raced out, spurred on by the king's command. And the edict was also issued in the citadel of Susa." The text emphasizes speed. These weren't ordinary horses—they were specially bred royal horses, the fastest available. The couriers raced out, spurred on by urgency.

Why the rush? Haman's decree had been sent out over two months earlier. People throughout the empire had already been preparing to attack the Jews. Some had probably been sharpening their weapons, making plans, choosing targets. The Jews, meanwhile, had been living under a death sentence with no hope of escape.

The sooner Mordecai's decree arrived, the sooner everything would change. Every day mattered. Every hour the new decree was delayed was another hour of hopelessness for Jewish communities scattered across 127 provinces.

So the horses ran as fast as they could carry the news: the Jews can fight back. The game has changed.

MORDECAI'S TRANSFORMATION

"Mordecai left the king's presence wearing royal garments of blue and white, a large crown of gold and a purple robe of fine linen. And the city of Susa held a joyous celebration."

Remember where we last saw Mordecai in mourning? He was wearing sackcloth and ashes, wailing in the streets, unable to enter the king's gate because of his clothes of grief. He looked like a man whose world was ending.

Now he emerges from the king's presence dressed like royalty. Blue and white—the royal colors of Persia. A golden crown. Purple linen. He looks like a man who runs an empire, because now he does.

And notice the city's response: Susa celebrated. Back when Haman's decree was issued, the text told us "the city of Susa was bewildered." The ordinary citizens knew something terrible was happening, even if they weren't sure why.

Now they celebrate. The people of Susa—Jews and non-Jews alike—rejoiced at Mordecai's rise to power. They understood that this change was good for everyone, not just the Jewish community.

JOY SPREADS

"For the Jews it was a time of happiness and joy, gladness and honor. And in every province and in every city, wherever the edict of the king went, there was joy and gladness among the Jews, with feasting and celebrating."

The author piles up words for joy: happiness, joy, gladness, honor, feasting, celebrating. After months of mourning and fasting, the Jewish communities throughout the empire finally had reason to hope.

Think about what this moment must have felt like. You're a Jewish family in some distant province. For months, you've been living under a death sentence. You've watched your neighbors look at you differently, knowing that soon they'll be legally permitted to kill you and take your stuff. You've wondered whether to run, to hide, to fight, to give up. You've held your children at night and wondered if they would survive.

And then a messenger arrives with news: you can fight back. The new prime minister is Jewish. The queen is Jewish. Everything has changed.

No wonder they feasted. No wonder they celebrated. The darkness wasn't completely gone—the day of confrontation was still coming. But for the first time in months, they could see a path forward.

OTHERS JOIN THE JEWS

The chapter ends with a surprising detail: "And many people of other nationalities became Jews because fear of the Jews had seized them." People from other ethnic groups started identifying as Jewish. Some scholars think this means full religious conversion—they adopted the Jewish faith and practices. Others think it means they allied themselves with the Jewish community politically, declaring themselves on the Jewish side of the coming conflict.

Either way, the reversal is stunning. Months earlier, Esther had hidden her Jewish identity because it seemed dangerous. Being known as a Jew was a liability—something that could get you killed. Now, being associated with the Jews seemed like the smart move. The balance of power had shifted so dramatically that non-Jews were choosing to join them.

"Fear of the Jews had seized them." This isn't necessarily a bad kind of fear. People could see that the Jewish God—though never named in the book—seemed to be protecting his people in remarkable ways. The whole series of events, from the king's sleepless night to Haman's execution on his own gallows, suggested that something or someone was watching over the Jews.

Haman's wife had predicted it: "Since Mordecai, before whom your downfall has started, is of Jewish origin, you cannot stand against him—you will surely come to ruin!" Even pagans could sense that the Jewish people had a protector they couldn't see.

WHAT THIS MEANS FOR US

First, defeating the villain doesn't always solve the problem. Haman was dead, but his evil lived on in the decree he created. Evil often works this way—it sets things in motion that continue even after the person responsible is gone. Cleaning up the damage often takes as much effort as stopping the initial harm.

Second, some wrongs can't be simply undone. The Persian legal system couldn't revoke its own laws. But that didn't mean nothing could be done. Mordecai found a creative solution—he couldn't erase the first decree, but he could write a second one that changed its practical effect. When we face situations that can't be simply reversed, we can still look for ways to counteract the damage and create new possibilities.

Third, position matters for justice. Mordecai couldn't have written his decree without the king's ring. Esther couldn't have approached the king without her position as queen. God had placed them exactly where they needed to be to help their people. The positions we hold—in our schools, our communities, our workplaces—aren't just for our own benefit. They might be exactly what's needed to help others when the moment comes.

Fourth, hope changes everything. The Jewish communities went from mourning to celebrating, from fasting to feasting. Their circumstances hadn't completely changed—the day of confrontation was still coming. But knowing they could fight back, knowing they weren't alone, transformed their experience. Sometimes just knowing there's a chance makes all the difference.

Fifth, God's people attract others. When it became clear that God was protecting the Jews, people wanted to join them. Faithfulness in hard times is a testimony that others notice. When we trust God through difficulties, we show the world something worth joining.

TALKING POINTS

Here are a few things to consider and talk over:

1. **The king couldn't revoke Haman's decree, so Mordecai**

had to write a new one to counter it. Can you think of situations where a problem couldn't be "undone" but could be counteracted? How do you find creative solutions when the obvious fix isn't available?

2. **Months earlier, being Jewish was dangerous—Esther had hidden her identity. Now people were choosing to identify with the Jews.** What changed? How does this show the difference between how things appear and how they actually are?

3. **The Jewish communities had to wait nine months between receiving the good news and actually facing the day of confrontation.** How do you handle waiting periods when you know something difficult is coming but you have reason to hope?

4. **Mordecai used the same ring that had sealed the death decree to seal the decree of defense.** What does it mean that the same tools can be used for very different purposes? How does this apply to positions of power or influence?

5. **The text says Esther fell at the king's feet and wept when asking him to stop Haman's plan.** Even after winning, she had to keep advocating for her people. Why is ongoing effort sometimes necessary even after a major victory?

The decree of death still stands. The decree of defense has been issued. Both will come into effect on the same day—the thirteenth of Adar. What will happen when those two laws collide?

Turn the page.

9

THE DAY THE TABLES TURNED

Every year on the Fourth of July, Americans celebrate Independence Day. There are fireworks and barbecues and parades. Families gather together, wave flags, and remember.

But what are they remembering? Most people at a July 4th celebration aren't thinking about the specific battles of the Revolutionary War. They're not reciting the Declaration of Independence word for word. They're celebrating something bigger: the story of how a group of colonies, facing a powerful empire, somehow won their freedom against all odds.

The celebration isn't just about the past. It's about identity. It says: "This is who we are. This is where we came from. We were once in danger, and we were delivered."

The Jewish people have a celebration like that too. It's called Purim, and it comes from the events in the book of Esther. Chapters 9–10 tell us what happened on the day the two decrees collided—and how that day became a festival that Jewish communities still celebrate thousands of years later.

The tables turned. And God's people never forgot it.

THE DAY ARRIVES

"On the thirteenth day of the twelfth month, the month of Adar, the edict commanded by the king was to be carried out. On this day the enemies of the Jews had hoped to overpower them, but now the tables were turned and the Jews got the upper hand over those who hated them."

Nine months of waiting were finally over. The thirteenth of Adar had arrived—the day Haman had chosen by casting lots, the day he thought would be "lucky" for destroying the Jews.

But the text tells us the outcome before it describes the events. The tables were turned. The Hebrew phrase literally means "it was reversed"—the exact opposite of what was expected happened. Those who planned to overpower the Jews were themselves overpowered. Those who hoped to destroy found themselves destroyed.

Notice something important: the text uses a passive verb. It doesn't say "the Jews turned the tables." It says the tables "were turned." The author is hinting, as he does throughout the book, that someone else was at work. The Jews defended themselves, but the reversal came from beyond their own strength.

WHAT ACTUALLY HAPPENED

"The Jews assembled in their cities in all the provinces of King Xerxes to attack those seeking their destruction. No one could stand against them, because the people of all the other nationalities were afraid of them."

Throughout the empire, Jews gathered together for defense. Remember Mordecai's decree—it gave them the right to assemble and protect themselves. That's exactly what they did.

The text says their enemies "could not stand against them." This doesn't mean there was no fighting. It means the fighting had a clear outcome. The people who chose to attack the Jews on this day found themselves facing organized resistance—and losing.

"And all the nobles of the provinces, the satraps, the governors and the king's administrators helped the Jews, because fear of Mordecai had seized them. Mordecai was prominent in the palace; his reputation spread throughout the provinces, and he became more and more powerful."

Here's a crucial detail: the government officials throughout the empire actively helped the Jews. Why? Because Mordecai was now the most powerful man in the kingdom after the king himself. Supporting the Jews meant supporting Mordecai. Opposing the Jews meant opposing the prime minister.

This is practical politics. When the power structure shifts, smart officials adjust their loyalties. Haman was dead. Mordecai was in charge. The wise choice was obvious.

But there's something else happening here. The phrase "fear of Mordecai" echoes language used elsewhere in the Bible for the "fear of God." The author may be hinting that what people were really sensing—even if they didn't recognize it—was the power of the God who stood behind Mordecai and his people.

THE NUMBERS

The text gives us specific numbers: "In the citadel of Susa, the Jews killed and destroyed five hundred men. They also killed ... the ten sons of Haman son of Hammedatha, the enemy of the Jews. But they did not lay their hands on the plunder."

In the capital city alone, five hundred enemies fell—plus Haman's ten sons, whose names are listed one by one. The sons had apparently continued their father's campaign against the Jews, even after his death. Now they met the same end he did.

The death toll throughout the empire was much larger: "Meanwhile, the remainder of the Jews who were in the king's provinces also assembled to protect themselves and get relief from their enemies. They killed seventy-five thousand of them but did not lay their hands on the plunder."

Seventy-five thousand is a staggering number. It tells us something important: the hatred against the Jews was far more widespread than we might have realized. Haman wasn't acting alone. His decree had unleashed something that was already present—a deep hostility that thousands of people throughout the empire were ready to act on when given permission.

The Jews weren't facing one villain. They were facing an empire-wide threat. And they survived.

WHAT THEY DIDN'T DO

Three times the text emphasizes something the Jews didn't do: "they did not lay their hands on the plunder." Mordecai's decree had given them permission to take the property of their enemies—the same permission Haman's decree had given to those who would attack Jews. But the Jews refused to take anything.

Why does this matter so much? In ancient Israel, there was a concept called "holy war"—battles fought not for personal gain but as agents of God's justice. One of the rules of holy war was that you didn't profit from it. You didn't take plunder. The victory belonged to God, not to you.

By refusing to take plunder, the Jews were signaling something: this wasn't about greed or revenge. This was about survival and justice. They weren't exploiting the situation for personal gain. They were defending their lives, nothing more.

The contrast with their enemies is striking. Haman's decree offered plunder as an incentive for attacking Jews. The whole scheme was motivated by greed and hatred. But the Jewish response was different. They took only what was necessary—their own survival—and left everything else.

A SECOND DAY

When the king heard the casualty report from Susa—five hundred enemies killed plus Haman's ten sons—he seemed almost impressed: "The king said to Queen Esther, 'The Jews have killed and destroyed five hundred men and the ten sons of Haman in the citadel of Susa. What have they done in the rest of the king's provinces? Now what is your petition? It will be given you. What is your request? It will also be granted.'"

Once again, the king offers Esther whatever she wants. And she makes one more request: "'If it pleases the king,' Esther answered, 'give the Jews in Susa permission to carry out this day's edict tomorrow also, and let Haman's ten sons be impaled on poles.'"

Esther asks for two things. First, she wants the Jews in Susa to have an extra day to defend themselves. The text doesn't explain why, but we can infer that the threat in the capital wasn't fully eliminated. Some enemies remained who would continue the attack if given the chance.

Second, she asks for Haman's sons to be publicly displayed. This wasn't additional killing—they were already dead. It was a public statement: the house of Haman is finished. Anyone still thinking of continuing his work should take note.

The king granted both requests. On the fourteenth of Adar, the Jews in Susa killed another three hundred enemies. Once again, they took no plunder.

FROM FIGHTING TO FEASTING

After the fighting ended, something beautiful happened: "This happened on the thirteenth day of the month of Adar, and on the fourteenth they rested and made it a day of feasting and joy. The Jews in Susa, however, had assembled on the thirteenth and fourteenth, and then on the fifteenth they rested and made it a day of feasting and joy."

The transition from battle to celebration was immediate. The day after the fighting stopped, the feasting began. The Jews throughout the provinces rested on the fourteenth and celebrated. The Jews in Susa, who had fought for two days, rested on the fifteenth and celebrated then.

This explains why Purim is celebrated on different days—the fourteenth of Adar in most places, the fifteenth in walled cities (following the pattern of Susa, which was a walled city). The celebration matches the history.

MAKING IT OFFICIAL

Mordecai didn't want this deliverance to be forgotten: "Mordecai recorded these things and sent letters to all the Jews in all the provinces of King Xerxes, near and far, to have them celebrate annually the fourteenth and fifteenth days of the month of Adar as the time when the Jews got relief from their enemies, and as the month when their sorrow was turned into joy and their mourning into a day of celebration."

Notice the language: sorrow turned into joy, mourning into celebration. This is the heart of Purim. It's not primarily a celebration of military victory. It's a celebration of reversal—of God taking a situation that looked hopeless and turning it completely around.

Mordecai gave instructions for how to celebrate: "He wrote them to observe the days as days of feasting and joy and giving presents of food to one another and gifts to the poor."

Purim was to be marked by three things: feasting (enjoying good food together), giving presents to friends (sharing joy with those you love), and giving gifts to the poor (making sure everyone could participate in the celebration, not just those who could afford it).

That last detail matters. Even in celebration, God's people were to remember those in need. Joy isn't complete when some are left out.

THE NAME "PURIM"

The festival got its name from an unexpected source: "Therefore these days were called Purim, from the word 'pur.' Because of everything written in this letter and because of what they had seen and what had happened to them, the Jews took it upon themselves to establish the custom that they and their descendants and all who join them should without fail observe these two days every year."

Remember the "pur"? It was the lot that Haman cast to choose the "lucky" day for destroying the Jews. It represented his pagan belief that fate or chance or random forces controlled the future.

The Jews named their festival after that lot—but with deep irony. The day chosen by casting lots became the day of their deliverance. The instrument of superstition became a reminder of providence. What looked like chance was actually the hand of God.

Every year when Jews celebrate Purim, the name itself proclaims: what Haman thought was luck was actually the sovereign plan of God. The lot is cast, but the decision belongs to the Lord.

ESTHER'S AUTHORITY

The book also emphasizes Esther's role in establishing Purim: "So Queen Esther, daughter of Abihail, along with Mordecai the Jew, wrote with full authority to confirm this second letter concerning Purim … The command of Queen Esther confirmed these regulations about Purim, and it was written down in the records."

Esther wasn't just a character in the story. She became an authority for her people. Her decree, along with Mordecai's, established Purim as an ongoing practice. A woman who had once hidden her Jewish identity was now using her royal authority to shape Jewish religious observance.

The orphan girl who was "taken" to the palace became the queen who wrote laws for her people. The reversal in Esther's personal life mirrored the reversal in her nation's fate.

THE EPILOGUE

The book ends with a brief note about what happened afterward: "King Xerxes imposed tribute throughout the empire, to its distant shores. And all his acts of power and might, together with a full account of the greatness of Mordecai, whom the king had promoted, are they not written in the book of the annals of the kings of Media and Persia? Mordecai the Jew was second in rank to King Xerxes, preeminent among the Jews, and held in high esteem by his many fellow Jews, because he worked for the good of his people and spoke up for the welfare of all the Jews."

Life returned to normal. The empire continued. Taxes were collected. Records were kept. But something had permanently changed: a Jew held the second-highest position in the most powerful empire on earth.

Mordecai used his power well. He didn't become corrupt or forget where he came from. He "worked for the good of his people and spoke up for the welfare of all the Jews." He remained faithful to his identity even at the height of his success.

The book ends not with the king but with Mordecai—reminding us that the real story was never about Persian politics. It was about God's faithfulness to his people through the faithfulness of individuals like Esther and Mordecai.

WHAT THIS MEANS FOR US

First, God's people are called to remember. Purim exists because Mordecai didn't want the deliverance to be forgotten. Memory matters. When we forget what God has done, we lose our sense of who we are and whose we are. Celebrations, traditions, and regular remembrance keep the story alive.

Second, celebration should include everyone. Purim wasn't just private joy—it included "gifts to the poor." True celebration makes room for those who might otherwise be left out. Our joy isn't complete while others are suffering.

Third, what looks like chance often isn't. The "pur"—the lot—was supposed to represent random fate. But the story shows that behind apparent randomness, God was working. The coincidences throughout Esther weren't coincidences at all. Neither are the unexpected turns in our own stories.

Fourth, deliverance is real but not final. The Jews were saved from Haman's plot, but they still lived in a pagan empire. Mordecai was powerful, but he would eventually die. The deliverance in Esther was wonderful and worth celebrating, but it pointed forward to something even greater—the ultimate deliverance that would come through another descendant of Abraham.

Fifth, ordinary people can shape history. Neither Esther nor Mordecai were prophets, priests, or kings of Israel. They were laypeople—a government official and a queen in a foreign court. Yet through their faithfulness in their ordinary positions, God accomplished extraordinary things. Your position in life isn't an obstacle to being used by God. It might be exactly where he's placed you for a purpose.

TALKING POINTS

Here are some points to consider and unpack together:

1. **The Jews celebrated their deliverance with feasting, giving presents to friends, and gifts to the poor.** Why do you think giving to the poor was included as part of the celebration? How does including others change the nature of joy?

2. **The festival was named after the "pur"—the lot Haman cast.** Why would the Jews name their celebration after something their enemy used? What does this say about how God can redeem even the plans of evil people?

3. **The book emphasizes three times that the Jews "did not lay their hands on the plunder."** Why was this detail so important? What does it tell us about the difference between justice and revenge?

4. **Mordecai used his position of power to work "for the good of his people."** How can people today use whatever influence they have—whether large or small—for the good of others?

5. **The book of Esther never directly mentions God, yet the whole story is about his protection of his people.** Why do you think the author wrote it this way? What does it teach us about how God often works in our lives?

The story began with a proud king throwing an extravagant party to display his own glory. It ends with a humble people celebrating together because someone greater than any king had protected them.

And every year, when the month of Adar comes around, Jewish communities still read this story aloud, still give gifts to friends and food to the poor, still remember the day the tables turned.

Because some stories are too important to forget.

The End.

www.ingramcontent.com/pod-product-compliance
Lightning Source LLC
Chambersburg PA
CBHW070125030426
42335CB00016B/2277